Karl Barth's Doubts about

Yaroslav Viazovski

Karl Barth's Doubts about John Calvin's Assurance

A Study of Two Doctrines of Assurance

VDM Verlag Dr. Müller

Impressum/Imprint (nur für Deutschland/ only for Germany)
Bibliografische Information der Deutschen Nationalbibliothek: Die Deutsche Nationalbibliothek verzeichnet diese Publikation in der Deutschen Nationalbibliografie; detaillierte bibliografische Daten sind im Internet über http://dnb.d-nb.de abrufbar.

Alle in diesem Buch genannten Marken und Produktnamen unterliegen warenzeichen-, marken- oder patentrechtlichem Schutz bzw. sind Warenzeichen oder eingetragene Warenzeichen der jeweiligen Inhaber. Die Wiedergabe von Marken, Produktnamen, Gebrauchsnamen, Handelsnamen, Warenbezeichnungen u.s.w. in diesem Werk berechtigt auch ohne besondere Kennzeichnung nicht zu der Annahme, dass solche Namen im Sinne der Warenzeichen- und Markenschutzgesetzgebung als frei zu betrachten wären und daher von jedermann benutzt werden dürften.

Coverbild: www.purestockx.com

Verlag: VDM Verlag Dr. Müller Aktiengesellschaft & Co. KG
Dudweiler Landstr. 99, 66123 Saarbrücken, Deutschland
Telefon +49 681 9100-698, Telefax +49 681 9100-988, Email: info@vdm-verlag.de

Herstellung in Deutschland:
Schaltungsdienst Lange o.H.G., Berlin
Books on Demand GmbH, Norderstedt
Reha GmbH, Saarbrücken
Amazon Distribution GmbH, Leipzig
ISBN: 978-3-639-21610-3

Imprint (only for USA, GB)
Bibliographic information published by the Deutsche Nationalbibliothek: The Deutsche Nationalbibliothek lists this publication in the Deutsche Nationalbibliografie; detailed bibliographic data are available in the Internet at http://dnb.d-nb.de .

Any brand names and product names mentioned in this book are subject to trademark, brand or patent protection and are trademarks or registered trademarks of their respective holders. The use of brand names, product names, common names, trade names, product descriptions etc. even without a particular marking in this works is in no way to be construed to mean that such names may be regarded as unrestricted in respect of trademark and brand protection legislation and could thus be used by anyone.

Cover image: www.purestockx.com

Publisher:
VDM Verlag Dr. Müller Aktiengesellschaft & Co. KG
Dudweiler Landstr. 99, 66123 Saarbrücken, Germany
Phone +49 681 9100-698, Fax +49 681 9100-988, Email: info@vdm-publishing.com

Copyright © 2009 by the author and VDM Verlag Dr. Müller Aktiengesellschaft & Co. KG and licensors
All rights reserved. Saarbrücken 2009

Printed in the U.S.A.
Printed in the U.K. by (see last page)
ISBN: 978-3-639-21610-3

Karl Barth's Doubts about John Calvin's Assurance:
A Comparison of Two Doctrines of Assurance

Yaroslav Viazovski

To Bill Patton

who made it possible

to get my first degree in theology

Table of Contents

Introduction — 7

Chapter 1. John Calvin — 11
    Scholarly Consensus and Disagreement — 11
    Formal Definition of Faith: Faith is Assurance — 16
    Beyond the Formal Definition: Assurance Coexists with Doubt — 33
    Conclusion — 41

Chapter 2. Karl Barth — 43
    Approach — 43
    The Doctrine of Election — 44
    The Problem of Universalism — 58
    The Doctrine of Assurance — 63
    A Broader Theological Context — 68
    Conclusion — 81

Chapter 3. A Comparative Analysis of Calvin's and Barth's Doctrines of Assurance — 85

Selected bibliography — 89

INTRODUCTION

The theme of this book is the assurance of salvation. It is certainly not of first rate doctrinal importance, yet it is not insignificant in theology and has special significance for the pastoral situation in which the present author finds himself.

Protestantism in Russia is still in its infancy. Today it is represented mainly by Baptists and Pentecostals whose congregations developed in the Russian Empire in the middle of the 19th century. Other Protestant denominations (e.g. Lutheran, Mennonite) have a longer history in this part of the world but their numbers and influence are negligible on the current religious scene, effectively making the evangelical movement (if we confine this term to Baptists and Pentecostals) in this country less than 200 years old. This leads to two consequences. First, the theology of the young Russian Protestantism as yet is unformed because nothing of theological importance has been written in Russian language so far. And second, the influence of the Russian Orthodox Church on the evangelical movement has always been strong.

As for the first consequence, there is currently no solid theological tradition in the form of theological literature with which modern Russian Baptists (including myself) can identify. Initially in the 19th century, Baptists ascribed to Calvinistic doctrines. But as time went by the situation has changed and now to be a Russian Baptist is to be a convinced Arminian. Obviously, one of the polarizing issues between Arminian Baptists (who are in majority) and Reformed Baptists (who have recently appeared on the scene about ten years ago and who are trying to return to what was believed in the 19th century) is the assurance of salvation, or to be more precise, the perseverance of the saints.

As for the second, there is a problem of complete lack of personal assurance of forgiveness of sins in Russian Orthodoxy. The Russian Orthodox theology, in spite of its long history, traceable to the work of John of Damascus' *The Exact Exposition of the Orthodox Faith* of the 8th century, is only partly developed. The overview of a number of older and more modern dogmatic theologies reveals an amazing fact: all dogma consists virtually only of three parts – the doctrine of creation (including providence and original sin), the doctrine of God (Christology included) and the doctrine of the church. Some textbooks add a section on the Bible and soteriology but these themes are only briefly touched on. There was only one attempt at systematic treatment of the doctrine of salvation at the end of 19th century in the form of a master's thesis which was later published as a book titled *The Orthodox Teaching on Salvation* by archbishop Sergii Stragorodski (1898) who in the beginning of the 20th century became the head of the Church. The author of this well-researched thesis begins with admission that he is the first theologian of the Russian Orthodox Church who ventures to present the doctrine of salvation systematically and in opposition to the Protestant teaching.

Since that time as far as the present author is aware there have been no similar books published. Nevertheless, the doctrine of salvation does exist in the Russian Orthodox Church. According to the *The Orthodox Teaching on Salvation* which represents the 'mainstream' theology of the Church the scheme of salvation is this. Jesus Christ came into the world to show us the true way of moral self-development. When we look at Him we see what kind of men we should be. In order to be saved we must take three steps. First, we should accomplish moral revolution in our souls and turn ourselves from sin to righteousness, from Satan to God. This is called regeneration. Second, we must take part in the sacrament of baptism in which divine grace strengthens our resolve to begin a new life. Third, we must strive for perfection and holiness in this life. It does not mean that only actual saints will go to heaven but

Introduction

it does mean that perfection is possible and that only those who have really striven and achieved considerable success will be saved at the end. The question remains: what about sins which we commit? The answer lies in the character of God: He is an all-loving and all-forgiving deity; therefore, He just closes His eyes to our sins when we turn to Him with resolve to become holy. That Christ is the sacrifice for our sins who redeems us from guilt is the terrible dogma of the medieval Roman Catholicism. That a man is justified by faith on the basis of Christ's righteousness imputed to him is the absurd invention of Luther.

This has obvious bearing on the issue of personal assurance. Since our salvation from the first to the last depends on our moral resolve and success in sanctification we cannot be sure of salvation until we die. In the end, the defining issue between the evangelical believers and the Russian Orthodox Christians is not the worship of icons or prayers for the dead but the possibility of personal assurance of salvation. Even more relevant is that this lack of assurance is common in the evangelical churches as well. The leaders of the Baptist churches constantly have to resist the influence of Russian Orthodox soteriology (if they themselves are not its victims).

One of the best ways to counteract this pastoral problem is to turn to the classical Reformed statements on the doctrine of assurance of salvation. Two representatives have been chosen for this purpose. One is John Calvin, the much maligned father of the Reformed movement, and despised by many Russian Baptists. The other is Karl Barth who is practically unknown among the Russian evangelicals but is important because he is a modern and original thinker who made a colossal attempt to restate the Reformed faith for the modern world.

1. JOHN CALVIN

Scholarly Consensus and Disagreement

John Calvin (1509-1564) was a great theologian. In spite of this fact, or perhaps exactly because of this fact, he left for the later generations a number of theological problems in his system. One of them is the relation between faith and assurance, which is the theme of this chapter. Is assurance a part of faith or one of its fruits? Can the true believer lack assurance or loose it after he has attained to it? What is the basis of assurance? The following overview of the scholarly discussion of the topic will lead us to formulation of the thesis which we will defend in this chapter.

James Packer believes that Calvin equated saving faith and assurance and that Puritans deviated from his teaching:

> For Luther, Zwingli, Bucer and Calvin, assurance was a normative component of faith. Calvin regarded saving faith as assurance of salvation, since he grounded assurance on Christ. Later Calvinism increasingly based assurance on sanctification, making it dependent on one's state of piety. Consequently, it was no longer regarded as an indispensable constituent element of saving faith. Correspondingly, the Westminster Confession of Faith (1647) separated saving faith and assurance into two non-contiguous chapters. Explanation for this change has been sought in factors such as the extent of the atonement and covenant theology (51).

William Cunningham (1805-1861) took a similar position to that of Packer regarding both Calvin's understanding of faith as assurance and the rejection of this doctrine by the later Calvinists. However Cunningham, explaining the origin of the

Karl Barth's Doubts about John Calvin's Assurance

Calvin's doctrine of assurance, gave a negative evaluation of it and approved of the change which had occurred in Puritan theology:

> The causes that tended to produce a leaning towards what may be regarded as exaggerated views and statements upon this subject [assurance], were chiefly these two: - 1st, Their own personal experience as converted and believing men; and, 2nd, The ground taken by the Romanists in arguing against them (113).

The first cause does not need further elaboration, it is sufficiently clear by itself. The second one deserves more attention. The basic objection which the Roman church put against the Reformers' doctrine of *Sola Scriptura* was that it takes away assurance. If it is not the church, but the Scripture which has authority over a believer's life, then there can be no certainty about canon, interpretation of Scripture and personal salvation. In response, the Reformers developed the doctrine of assurance based on the work of the Holy Spirit.

> The Reformers claimed for their convictions and conclusions, on these questions [canon, interpretation, salvation] a kind and degree of certainty which the nature of the subject did not admit of, and they fell into further errors in endeavoring to set forth the grounds or reasons of the certainty or assurance for which they contended. They contended that they had, or might have, a perfect and absolute certainty in regard to all those matters, - a certainty resting not only upon rational grounds and a human faith, as it was called, but upon supernatural grounds and a divine faith, such as their popish opponents were accustomed to ascribe to the authority of the church, when it set forth any doctrine and called upon men to believe it as revealed by God. And as a substitute for the authority of the church, the popish ground for an absolute assurance and divine faith, the Reformers were accustomed to bring in the agency of the Holy Spirit, as producing certainty or assurance (Cunningham 115-116).

From Cunningham's point of view there can be no doubt that the Reformers and in particular Calvin equated faith and assurance:

John Calvin

The Reformers, in order to show that the assurance which might be attained without either a special revelation or the testimony of the church, was full and perfect, were led to identify it with our belief in the doctrine of God's word, and to represent it as necessarily included or implied in the act or exercise of justifying and saving faith; nay, even sometimes to give it as the very definition of saving faith, that it is a belief that our own sins have been forgiven and that we have been brought into a state of grace... Calvin had undoubtedly taught in his 'Institutes,' and also in his 'Catechism' of Geneva, that saving faith necessarily includes or implies personal assurance (118, 124).

Having stated Calvin's understanding, first, of the witness of the Spirit as the basis of assurance and, second, of the relation between faith and assurance, Cunningham demonstrates that 'This view was certainly exaggerated and erroneous' (119). We think his considerations are important for the correct understanding of Calvin himself but at the same time we hope to show that Calvin's doctrine is still valid in spite of the apparently devastating critique by Cunningham. He presents two basic objections to Calvin's doctrine of assurance. First, he objects to the idea that assurance is based on the work of the Holy Spirit:

It is very evident that no man can be legitimately assured of his own salvation simply by understanding and believing what is contained or implied in the actual statements of Scripture. Some additional element of a different kind must be brought in, in order to warrant such an assurance; something in the state or condition of the man himself must be in some way ascertained and known in order to this result. It may not, indeed always require any lengthened or elaborate process of self-examination to ascertain what is needful to be known about men themselves, in order to their being assured that they have been brought into a state of grace... And when they are called upon to state and vindicate to themselves or to others the grounds of their assurance, they must of necessity proceed, in substance, in the line of the familiar syllogism, 'Whosoever believeth in the Lord Jesus Christ shall be saved; I believe, and therefore,' etc... (118).

The argument seems to be very convincing: it is one thing to believe that any believer is saved, it is another thing to know that I am saved. I can be sure that I am saved

Karl Barth's Doubts about John Calvin's Assurance

only if I know that I believe in Christ's promises. But Calvin, as we will show later, teaches that if a man has saving faith then as soon as he comes to believe that the promises of Christ are true in general, Holy Spirit gives him assurance that these promises are applied to him personally. Thus, man does not need to reason in a syllogistic way: the Holy Spirit gives him assurance apart from the syllogism. Cunningham is right: from the point of view of logic syllogistic way of reasoning is indispensable for obtaining assurance. Nevertheless Calvin is also right because he looks at the issue of assurance not from the point of view of logic but from the point of view of the work of the Holy Spirit. Unlike Cunningham, Calvin recognizes activity of the Holy Spirit who can work in our minds apart from syllogistic reasoning. 'Even in its noetic aspect, faith is not for Calvin, the approval of propositions about God, but an existential awareness' (Dowey 204). For Cunningham the Spirit cannot work in this way, and that is why he criticizes Calvin. But if one can accept Calvin's idea of the assurance born through the word and the work of the Spirit for him Cunningham's first objection is answered.

Secondly, Cunningham objects to the idea that assurance is included in faith:

> It is unwarrantable to give as the definition of saving faith, the belief that my sins are forgiven; for it is not true that my sins are forgiven until I believe, and it holds true universally, that God requires us to believe nothing which is not true before we believe it, and which may not be propounded to us to be believed, accompanied as the time with satisfactory evidence of its truth; and if so, the belief that our sins are forgiven, and that we have been brought into a state of grace, must be posterior in the order of nature, if not of time, to the act of faith by which the change is effected, and cannot therefore form a necessary constituent element of the act itself, cannot be its essence or belong to its essence (119).

Actually Cunningham only repeats what Puritans taught long before him. For instance, the 17th century Puritan Thomas Brooks proves that assurance cannot be part of faith reasoned in the same way:

John Calvin

> A man must first be saved before he can be assured of his salvation, for he cannot be assured of that which is not; and a man must have saving grace before he can be saved, for he cannot be saved by that which he hath not. Again, a man must be ingrafted into Christ, before he can be assured of remission or salvation, but this cannot be before he hath faith... (337).

However, this objection can be answered too. Cunningham misuses logic: for him we cannot be sure in forgiveness of our sins before we are forgiven therefore assurance cannot be a part of faith. He does not notice that in this context there is no difference between assurance that my sins *are* forgiven and that they *will be* forgiven because it is God who promises forgiveness. It is true that when we come to faith in Christ we are not forgiven yet. But we can be sure even before we have actually received forgiveness that we will be forgiven because Christ's promise cannot fail. How many times David in his psalms praised God for his help even before God had helped him? And did not apostle Paul say that those who are predestined, called and justified are glorified as well? If Calvin is guilty of a logical fallacy in his definition of faith than David and Paul are guilty of the same fallacy.

Joel Beeke looks at the problem of faith and assurance in Calvin's thought from a different angle. Unlike Cunningham, he does not ask how we can be assured of forgiveness of our sins before we are forgiven. For Beeke the problem is this: Calvin seems to teach that a true believer must have full assurance while admitting that the believer inevitably has doubts. In words of Beeke himself:

> How could Calvin say that assertions of faith are characterized by full assurance, yet still allow for the kind of faith that lacks assurance? The two statements appear antithetical. Assurance is free from doubts, yet not free. It does not hesitate, yet can hesitate; it contains security, but may be beset with anxiety; the faithful have assurance, yet waver and tremble (44).

Beeke points out four principles which help to resolve the apparent paradox in Calvin's thought. First, faith and experience; 'Calvin distinguished between the "*ought to*" of faith in its essence, and the "*is*" of faith as wrestled out in daily life' (45). Second, flesh versus spirit; 'Calvin teaches that from *the spirit* of the believer rise hope, joy, assurance; from *the flesh*, fear, doubt, disillusionment. Though spirit and flesh operate simultaneously, Calvin maintained that imperfection and doubt are integral only to the flesh, not to faith. The works of the flesh often *attend* faith, but do not *mix* with it' (51). Third, the germ of faith versus consciousness of faith; 'Calvin [taught] that the smallest germ of faith contains assurance in its essence, even when the believer is not always able to grasp this assurance due to a weak consciousness of his faith' (51). 'Through a fourth sweeping principle, namely, a *Trinitarian framework* for the doctrines of faith and assurance, Calvin intended to spur forward believers who are prone to doubt. As surely as the *election* of the Father must prevail over the works of Satan; the *righteousness* of the Son over the sinfulness of the believer; the *assuring witness* of the Spirit over the soul's infirmities – so certainly assured faith shall and must conquer doubt and unbelief' (55).

While all three scholars agree that for Calvin assurance belonged to the essence of faith they give different evaluation of this doctrine. Cunningham believed it to be erroneous and self-contradictory, Beeke thinks that Calvin's teaching is valid if understood in the full context of Calvin's thought. In this chapter we follow Beeke's suggestion and work out the following thesis*: for Calvin, assurance, which is inseparable from faith, is present in the true believer from the very beginning of his spiritual life and never leaves him in spite of the reality of doubts, fear and anxiety.*

Formal Definition of Faith: Faith Is Assurance

Definition

Calvin gives the following definition of faith: it 'is a firm and sure knowledge, of the divine favor toward us, founded on the truth of a free promise in Christ, and revealed to our minds, and sealed on our hearts, by the Holy Spirit' (III.2.7)[1]. In this definition Calvin as clearly as possible includes assurance of personal salvation in the concept of faith. For him faith is assurance. Calvin's clarity at this point explains the scholarly

---

[1] When quoting from Calvin's *Institutes* we give only numbers at the end of quotation: book, chapter, section in the chapter. The quotations are taken from Battles' translation of *Institutes* unless other translation is indicated.

consensus about his understanding of assurance as being a part of faith. Later in the same chapter of *Institutes* he elaborates each phrase of this definition showing its biblical character and explaining how it can be harmonized with the real experience of believers. In discussing his understanding of assurance below, we follow his method.

Knowledge

For Calvin, faith is not feeling but knowledge. He points out the difference between two kinds of knowledge (III.2.14). One can be achieved by 'human sense', by 'its [mind's] own capacity', by 'demonstration of reason'. The other 'surpasses all understanding [i.e. knowledge in the first sense]', it is achieved 'by a belief of the divine veracity', and comes 'from mere certainty of persuasion'. In other words, the first kind of knowledge is the result of natural thinking, it is a matter of 'discernment', as we say today of 'scientific thinking'. The second kind of knowledge is based on revelation from God and belief in God's truthfulness. Faith is the second kind of knowledge. By *faith* we should understand that *knowledge* which we obtain not by reasoning but by accepting revelation from God.

From Calvin's point of view, faith is far from being an inferior kind of knowledge and is in fact superior to the 'scientific knowledge' because 'it understands more from mere certainty of persuasion than it could discern of any human matter by its own capacity' (III.2.14). It is sometimes claimed that faith is not real knowledge because it is not based on direct observation and cannot be verified[2]. While this fact must be admitted it should be pointed out that in spite of seemingly inferior method of obtaining knowledge faith gives man knowledge which exceeds his rational capacities to know. Reason can never give us knowledge of grace in Christ but faith can and does. Therefore, for Calvin, assurance, which he equates with faith, cannot be based on syllogistic reasoning because the latter may be applied only

---

[2] For example a nineteenth-century mathematician W. K. Clifford in his essay *The Ethics of Belief* states: 'It is wrong always, everywhere, and for anyone, to believe anything upon insufficient evidence" (quoted in Ronald H. Nash, *Faith and Reason: Searching for a Rational Faith*, Grand Rapids, MI: Zondervan, 1988).

to 'human matter'. We cannot be sure that we are forgiven by God on the basis of syllogism. Only the Spirit who works through the word of revelation can give assurance of personal salvation. To underscore this fact Calvin says: 'From this we conclude that the knowledge of faith consists in assurance rather than in comprehension' (III.2.14).

The following diagram shows the limitations of syllogistic reasoning: it cannot serve as a basis of assurance of divine favor to us because the latter does not belong to 'human matter', it is a matter of revelation.

	Knowledge	**Faith-knowledge**
Method	Demonstration of reason	Acceptance of God's revelation
Content	Human matter	God's favor to us

Faith is knowledge which is sure and firm. 'For as faith is not contented with a dubious and fickle opinion [sure], so neither is it contented with obscure and ill-defined conception [firm]' (III.2.15). From such understanding of faith as sure and firm knowledge follows discussion of two reasons why assurance may be lacking.

1. Doubting God's veracity. 'So deeply rooted in our hearts is unbelief, so prone are we to it, that while all confess with the lips that God is faithful, no man ever believes it without arduous struggle' (III.2.15). To fight this 'perverse doubt' God witnesses many times in his word that his word is true (e.g. Pss. 12:6; 18:30; 30:5; 119).

2. Misunderstanding of God's mercy. 'There are very many also who form such an idea of the divine mercy as yields them very little comfort' (III.2.15). In particular, a person may seem to believe that God is infinitely merciful but at the same time may be uncertain whether he can obtain this mercy or not. True faith excludes this fault: 'Very different is that feeling of full assurance (*plerophoria*) which the Scriptures uniformly attribute to faith – an assurance that leaves no doubt that the goodness of God is clearly offered to us' (III.2.15). Then Calvin, referring to

Eph. 3:12, says: '...[O]ur faith is not true unless it enables us to appear calmly in the presence of God' (III.2.15). He makes the same conclusion after citing each of the following Scriptural passages: Rom. 1:5; Heb. 3:14; Rom. 8:38; Eph. 1:18. The entire paragraph (III.2.16) is emphatic denial of faith without assurance: 'none hope well', 'no man is a believer', 'eyes of our understanding are not enlightened', 'goodness of God is not properly comprehended' – if 'security does not follow as its fruit'.

For Calvin then, true faith not only gives us knowledge content which supersedes our natural capacity to know, it gives us certainty which is unattainable by 'scientific methods' because all human conclusions can be subject to doubt while God's word cannot be questioned. However, on the way to this 'sure and firm knowledge' there is the twofold barrier of doubting God's veracity and misunderstanding of his mercy. Only that person has true faith who accepting God's word as ultimate truth believes that God is merciful to him personally.

Free Promise

'Faith has no less need of the word than the fruit of a tree has of a living root' (III.2.31). When Calvin says 'the word' in the context of the discussion of faith and assurance he mainly means promise. The special object of faith is God's promise. While this statement does not deny that the believer accepts all the words of God it affirms that until the promise of grace is grasped faith is not true faith. 'We only mean to maintain these two points, – that faith is never decided until it attain to a free promise; and that the only way in which faith reconciles us to God is by uniting us with Christ' (III.2.30).

God's promise is not only the object of faith but at the same time it is its foundation. Faith 'properly begins with promise, continues with it, and ends with it' (III.2.29). Only free promise can give life to faith:

> And this promise must be gratuitous; for a conditional promise, which throws us back upon our works, promises life only in so far as we find it existing in ourselves. Therefore, if we would not have faith to waver and tremble, we must

support it with the promise of salvation, which is offered by the Lord spontaneously and freely, from regard to our misery, rather than our worth (III.2.29).

As soon as we abandon the free promise and try to find any other foundation for faith we loose assurance: we cannot be sure of our salvation if we rely, for example, on our sanctification. The free promise is the only ground for assurance. The scholastic dogma says 'that we can have no stronger evidence of the divine favor toward us than moral conjecture, according as each individual deems himself not unworthy of it' (III.2.38). Calvin carries this thought to its logical conclusion: 'Doubtless, if we are to determine by our works in what way the Lord stands affected toward us, I admit that we cannot even get the length of a feeble conjecture' (III.2.38). To say that God gives us free promise of salvation is the same as saying that God establishes a gracious covenant with sinners therefore we should look at the covenant as foundation of our assurance. Commenting on the words 'I will not violate my covenant or alter what my lips have uttered' from Ps. 89:34 Calvin says:

> As the true knowledge of God's mercy can only be obtained from his word, he enjoins us to keep our eyes intently fixed upon his covenant. The more excellent and invaluable a blessing it is, "Never to be rejected after having been once adopted by him," the more difficult it is for us to believe its truth. And we know how many thoughts from time to time present themselves to our minds, tempting us to call it in question. That the faithful, therefore, may not harass themselves beyond measure in debating in their own minds whether or not they are in favour with God, they are enjoined to look to the covenant, and to embrace the salvation which is offered to them in it. God here commends to us his own faithfulness, that we may account his promise sufficient, and that we may not seek the certainty of our salvation anywhere else (*Heart Aflame* 214).

For one thing, it is the word in which the promise is given to us therefore the word is crucial for faith. But the word also discloses to us the power of God. Though it seems trivial to believe in God's might the prophets did not magnify it in vain. 'Unless the power of God, to which all things are possible, is presented to our eye, our ears malignantly refuse admission to the word [of promise] or set no just value upon it'

(III.2.38). Besides, the word discloses to us God's power as actively caring power. The Prophets constantly reminded ancient Israel about the Exodus from Egypt because this was an example of great display of divine power for the sake of God's people. Examples of Sarah and Rebekah show importance of the word for faith. On the one hand, their very inordinate zeal was prompted by faith in God's promise, on the other hand, they did not rely on promise fully enough. From this fact Calvin draws two conclusions: one about inevitable triumph of faith and the other about dependence of faith on the word. 'These examples certainly show that error is often mingled with faith; and yet that when faith is real it always obtains preeminence' (III.2.38). 'Still they admonish us how carefully we ought to cling to the word of God, and at the same time confirm what we have taught – viz. that faith gives way when not supported by the word...' (III.2.38). Thus the word which contains the promise of the divine favor and witnesses to the divine power is the one necessary foundation for faith and assurance.

Finally, we should point out that for Calvin faith and assurance depend on the fact that the Bible is the very word of God, the word which is infallible and self-authenticated. The Scripture which errs or is subject to the judgment of men is a shaky ground for assurance.

> When that which is forth is acknowledged to be the Word of God, there is no one so deplorably insolent...as to dare impugn the credibility of Him who speaks. Now daily oracles are not sent from heaven, for it pleased the Lord to hallow his truth to everlasting remembrance in the Scriptures alone. Hence the Scriptures obtain full authority among believers only when men regard them as having sprung from heaven, as if the living words of God were heard... [W]hat will happen to miserable consciences seeking firm assurance of eternal life if all promises of it consist in and depend solely upon the judgment of men? (I.7.1).

Karl Barth's Doubts about John Calvin's Assurance

Spirit

Without God's word there can be no assurance, but the word itself is ineffective without the Spirit. 'A simple external manifestation of the word ought to be amply sufficient to produce faith, did not our blindness and perverseness prevent' (III.2.33). Our mind 'is always blind even in his light. Hence without illumination of the Spirit the word has no effect' (III.2.33).

> The word is, in regard to those to whom it is preached, like the sun which shines upon all, but is of no use to the blind. In this matter we are all naturally blind; and hence the word cannot penetrate our mind unless the Spirit, that internal teacher, by his enlightening power make an entrance for it (III.2.34).

One of the first works of the Holy Spirit in this regard is to make men to renounce 'human discernment [which] is so defective and lost' (III.2.34.). The Spirit not only initiates faith in us but also supports it and gives it growth.

> Faith is the special gift of God in both ways, - in purifying the mind so as to give it a relish for divine truth, and afterwards in establishing it... The Spirit performs the part of a seal, sealing upon our hearts the very promises, the certainty of which was previously impressed upon our minds (III.2.33).

It is not completely clear what Calvin means here by the sealing of the heart. Our minds not only know God's promises in Christ, but due to the illumination of the Spirit they know it certainly. What then is the purpose of sealing of our hearts? To make certainty even more certain? To give certainty to our emotions? To give certainty that God's promises in Christ are given personally to me?

We may answer the question, if we turn, for instance, to his sermon on Ephesians 1:13-14. But even before we quote from that sermon we may already draw an important conclusion: for Calvin it is not syllogistic reasoning which gives us certainty of faith but the Holy Spirit who illumines our minds to see the truthfulness of God's promise in Christ and seals our heart. And what exactly sealing of the heart by the Spirit means we may gather from the following passage:

Now, there is yet another point, which is that when we have once embraced God's grace by faith, so that we know that our Lord Jesus Christ is he in whom we find all that is required to make us perfectly happy, it is very necessary for us to be established in this truth. And why? Let us notice how volatile men are. He that is best disposed to follow God will soon fall, for we are so frail that the devil will overcome us every minute of time, if God does not hold us up with a strong hand... Thus God's Spirit does a twofold work in us with respect to faith. For he enlightens us to make us understand things which otherwise would be hidden from us, and to receive God's promises with all obedience. That is the first part of his work. The second is that the same Spirit is pleased to abide in us and to give us perseverance, that we do not draw back in the midst of our way... That, therefore, is the reason why he [St. Paul] says here that they were sealed by the Holy Spirit (*Sermons on Ephesians* 73).

The sealing of the Spirit is nothing else but the gift of perseverance in faith. Without the twofold work of the Spirit we could neither believe nor keep our faith and assurance. The syllogistic approach to assurance is a blind alley in spiritual counseling of Puritans because it overestimates the spiritual ability of men to believe and underestimates the power of doubts which arise both from our own hearts and are inspired in us from without by Satan and the world. Calvin trusts the sovereign operation of God the Holy Spirit who gives and establishes faith and refuses to domesticate and control Him by legalistic approach to assurance based on sanctification. From his point of view we should look for strengthening of assurance only in the word of God trusting at the same time that the Spirit of God will work through the word.

In Christ

All promises which we ever receive from God he gives us in Christ (2 Cor 1:20). No promise is given outside of Christ. 'God loves no man out of Christ' (III.2.32). Examples of Naaman, the eunuch in Acts, and Cornelius do not contradict this assertion because there is sufficient evidence that each one of them knew something of the promise about Christ. Naaman knew from Elisha, the eunuch knew probably from the Scripture, and Cornelius knew from the Jews among which he lived. 'I admit that, in some respect, their faith was not explicit either as to the person of Christ, or the power and office assigned him by the Father. Still it is certain that they were imbued with principles which might give some, though a slender, foretaste of Christ' (III.2.32). Thus, faith is not general knowledge about God's mercy but is sure and firm knowledge of God's mercy given to us in Christ.

The phrase 'in Christ' not only indicates that the object of faith is the person and work of Christ but also implies that we are accepted by God on the basis of the union with Christ: '…the only way in which faith reconciles us to God is by uniting us with Christ' (III.2.30). We can be sure of salvation because and only because we know that we are in Christ. For Calvin, without union with Christ we could never be perfect enough to be accepted by God. Only reminding ourselves that we are 'in Christ' we can be assured of salvation.

To underscore the importance of Calvin's teaching that we have assurance only in Christ we may compare it to the Puritan approach to the problem of the lack of assurance. For instance, from point of view of Thomas Brooks, lack of assurance may be explained by a number of similar reasons. One of them is the 'cavilling spirit' (338) of the believer. It is as if the Christian does not want to see the graces which are in him. The lack of assurance may also arise from 'the exceeding littleness and weakness of his grace' (338). Believer's old sins may resurface or he may fall short of 'that perfection that the word requires' (339). Fear and doubts raised by corruption hide graces from the sight and they cannot be discerned (340). Lastly, when the believer does not search and examine his soul he cannot see God's work in his heart and therefore cannot have assurance (340-341).

For Brooks moral life is the sole foundation of assurance. If the Christian does not have assurance the cause must be in himself. He either does not produce sufficient evidence of sanctification, or does not notice his own graces, or is overwhelmed by his corruption, or falls into old sins. In one word from the Puritan perspective assurance totally depends on the subjective state of the believer and his discernment of this state. If one wants assurance he must look to himself.

But Calvin makes believers to be totally dependent on Christ: not only in salvation but also in assurance of salvation. We cannot rely on our spiritual achievements because they are meager. Only looking at ourselves as being in Christ we can be sure of salvation. Calvin says:

> Yet more: we experience such participation in him that although we are still foolish in ourselves, he is our wisdom before God; while we are sinners, he is our righteousness; while we are unclean, he is our purity; while we are weak, while we are unarmed and exposed to Satan, yet ours is that power which has been given him in heaven and upon earth, by which to crush Satan for us and shatter the gates of hell; while we still bear about with us the body of death, he is yet our life (III.15.5).

As soon as we stop looking to Christ as the foundation of God's favor to us and begin to examine our souls in attempt to find holiness within ourselves we loose wisdom, righteousness, purity, strength, life. By faith we are united to Christ and by faith we know that 'we have all things in him, in us there is nothing' (III.15.5).

However Calvin does not disregard the moral life of the believer completely. He gives it a role to play in the experience of assurance. He looks at our sanctification as the secondary means of assurance. Commenting on the words of Psalm 119:159, 'See how I love your precepts; preserve my life, O Lord, according to your love', Calvin says:

> When the saints speak of their own piety before God they are not chargeable with obtruding their own merits as the ground of their own confidence; but they regard this as a settled principle, that God, who distinguishes his servants from the profane and wicked, will be merciful to them because they seek him with their whole heart. Besides, an unfeigned love of God's law is an undoubted evidence of adoption, since this love is the work of the Holy Spirit. The prophet, therefore, although he arrogates nothing to himself, very properly adduces his own piety for the purpose of encouraging himself to entertain the

more ensured hope of obtaining his request, through the grace of God which he had experienced' (*Heart Aflame* 328).

We should notice that Calvin is somewhat embarrassed by the fact that the psalmist speaks about his love for the law of God as the basis of his confidence in prayer. He concedes that 'unfeigned love of God's law is an undoubted evidence of adoption, since this love is the work of the Holy Spirit' and then simply states that his piety is encouragement for the more ensured hope. We may compare this reserved statement with his insistence on the word as the sole foundation of faith and assurance ('Faith has no less need of the word than the fruit of a tree has of a living root', faith 'properly begins with promise, continues with it, and ends with it' etc.) and conclude that for him personal piety was not as crucial for assurance as the promise.

In his commentary on 1 John 2:3 Calvin contrasts grace of Christ and our works and underlines that the foundation of faith is the former not the latter:

> 'If we keep his commandments'... But we are not hence to conclude that faith recumbs on works; for though every one receives a testimony to his faith from his works, yet it does not follow that it is founded on them, since they are added as an evidence. Then the certainty of faith depends on the grace of Christ alone; but piety and holiness of life distinguish true faith from theft knowledge of God which is fictitious and dead; for the truth is, that those who are in Christ, as Paul says, have put off the old man.

The works fulfill a negative function: they 'distinguish true faith from theft knowledge of God'. The good works or rather the lack thereof protects true believers from presumption and alert nominal Christians to their true condition but they are not the foundation on which assurance can be based.

Election

One may expect that the doctrine of election for which Calvin's name is both admired and hated plays an important role in the assurance of salvation. However we find in

John Calvin

Calvin something very different from what might have been expected. He could have reasoned in the following way: I know that I am one of God's elect therefore I am sure of my salvation. But Calvin is true to his doctrine of assurance based on the free promise in Christ and vehemently rejects the proposed syllogism. Election is not the foundation of assurance, rather knowledge of election is posterior to obtaining of assurance.

Election is actually hidden from us in God until God calls us to Christ: '...God by his call manifests the election, which he otherwise holds hidden within himself...' (III.24.1). We know about our election only after conversion. Only the fact that we are called and justified discloses to us the eternal decision of God to choose us for salvation: 'Now among the elect we regard the call as a testimony of election. Then we hold justification another sign of its manifestation, until they come into the glory in which the fulfillment of that election lies... the Lord seals his elect by call and justification...' (III.21.7).

Since we cannot know about our election apart from our calling and justification it is wrong to base assurance on knowledge of election which is obtained in a different way. In no uncertain words, Calvin condemns the wrong way of seeking the certainty of election.

> [W]e shall be following the best order if, in seeking the certainty of our election, we cling to those latter signs [call, justification] which are sure attestations of it. Satan has no more grievous or dangerous temptation to dishearten believers than when he unsettles them with doubt about their election, while at the same time he arouses them with a wicked desire to seek it outside the way. I call it "outside the way" when mere man attempts to break into the inner recesses of divine wisdom, and tries to penetrate even the highest eternity, in order to find out what decision has been made concerning himself at God's judgment seat. For then he casts himself into the depth of a bottomless whirlpool to be swallowed up...
>
> Rare indeed is the mind that is not repeatedly struck with this thought: whence comes your salvation but from God's election? Now, what revelation do you have of your election? This thought, if it has impressed itself upon him,

either continually strikes him in his misery with harsh torments or utterly overwhelms him... For just as those engulf themselves in a deadly abyss who, to make their election more certain, investigate God's eternal plan apart from his Word, so those who rightly and duly examine it as it is contained in his Word reap the inestimable fruit of comfort. Let this, therefore, be the way of our inquiry: to begin with God's call, and to end with it (III.24.4).

The overarching doctrine of the union with Christ plays an important role in Calvin's doctrine of election and brings us back to the fundamental idea that assurance should be sought in Christ and not in ourselves. Calvin uses the image of a mirror to describe how the union with Christ functions in respect of election. Christ is 'the mirror' of our election in two important senses. First, we do not deserve to be chosen for salvation. We are elected only in Christ who is the mirror at which God looked when he decided to elect us.

Did God, then, have an eye to us when he vouchsafed to love us? No! No! for then he would have utterly abhorred us. It is true that in regarding our miseries he had pity and compassion on us to relieve us, but that was because he had already loved us in our Lord Jesus Christ. God, then, must have had before him his pattern and mirror in which to see us, that is to say, he must have first looked on our Lord Jesus Christ before he could choose and call us (*Sermons on Ephesians* 33).

[I]f we seek God's fatherly mercy and kindly heart, we should turn our eyes to Christ... [T]hose whom God has adopted as his sons are said to have been chosen not in themselves but in Christ; for unless he could love them in him, he could not honor them with the inheritance of his Kingdom if they had not previously become partakers of him. But if we have been chosen in him, we shall not find assurance of our election in ourselves; and not even in God the Father, if we conceive him as severed from his Son (III.24.5).

Second, election is hidden from us but Christ is 'the mirror' in which election is revealed to us. We should look at Christ if we want be certain of our election.

Christ, then, is the mirror wherein we must, and without self-deception may, contemplate our own election... How insane are we to seek outside him what we have already obtained in him, and can find in him alone? Moreover, since he is the eternal wisdom of the Father, his unchangeable truth, his firm counsel, we ought not to be afraid of what he tells us in his Word varying in the slightest from that will of the Father which we seek. Rather, he faithfully reveals to us that will as it was from the beginning and ever shall be (III.24.5).

How do we know that God has elected us before the creation of the world? By believing in Jesus Christ. I said before that faith proceeds from election and is the fruit of it, which shows that the root is hidden within. Whosoever then believes is thereby assured that God has worked in him, and faith is, as it were, the duplicate copy that God gives us of the original of our adoption...

You see then that the faith which we have in our Lord Jesus Christ is enough to assure us of our election, and therefore, what more do we ask? I told you that Jesus Christ is the mirror in which God beholds us when he wishes to find us acceptable to himself. Likewise, on our side, he is the mirror on which we must cast our eyes and look, when we desire to come to the knowledge of our election (*Sermons on Ephesians* 48).

Thus, on the one hand, Christ is the source, the foundation, the root of our election. On the other hand, he is the revelation, disclosure and the certainty of it. If we thought that God had chosen us for something in ourselves we could not be sure of our election because there is nothing constantly good and deserving in us. But we find peace in our minds knowing that God has chosen us 'in Christ', in whom dwells goodness and who deserves to be elected. Furthermore, we could not be certain of our election if Christ did not reveal it to us by means of the promise of salvation given personally to us. In other words, his personal effectual call by which he gives us faith opens to us the otherwise forever hidden decree of God. So we see that from Calvin's point of view election is not a basis of assurance in salvation. Rather, faith in God's promise (which includes assurance of salvation) is the certainty of our election. However, in a sense election *is* a foundation of assurance and to this thought we now turn.

Karl Barth's Doubts about John Calvin's Assurance

Assurance of the future

It should be pointed out that for Calvin faith is assurance not only of *present* reconciliation with God but also of *future* eternal life. He does not separate the promise of forgiveness from the promise of perseverance. These are not two distinct promises but one great blessing given by our gracious God. The gift of perseverance is included in the promise of salvation on which faith rests. To have faith is to have firm and sure knowledge of the present favor of God and of possession of the gift of perseverance.

> The divine favour to which faith is said to have respect, we understand to include in it the possession of salvation and eternal life. For if, when God is propitious, no good thing can be wanting to us, we have ample security for our salvation when assured of his love... When God is reconciled all danger is past, and everything good will befell us... the chief security lies in the expectation of future life, which is placed beyond doubt by the word of God (III.2.28).

Election is the guarantee of our future salvation. Calvin masterfully defines election in Johannine terms in order to show that the elect cannot fall away. According to the gospel of John election is nothing else but giving of people by God the Father to God the Son for the purpose of care and protection. Therefore if we are elect, our present reconciliation with God will be inevitably consummated in eternity.

> The fact that, as we said, the firmness of our election is joined to our calling is another means of establishing our assurance. For those whom Christ has illumined with the knowledge of his name and has introduced into the bosom of his church, he is said to receive into his care and keeping. All whom he receives, the Father is said to have entrusted and committed to him to keep unto eternal life. What would we have? Christ proclaims aloud that he has taken under his protection all whom the Father wishes to be saved. Therefore, if we desire to know whether God cares for our salvation, let us inquire whether he has entrusted us to Christ, whom he has established as the sole Saviour of all his people (III.24.6).

John Calvin

If Christ starts good work in us he cannot fail to continue and complete it. He will not forsake the work of his own hands. He prays for all the elect that their faith may never fall. His care gives us such assurance that we are able 'to lord over life and death, things present and to come' (III.24.6). After quoting a number of biblical texts which show that election implies Christ's care and the gift of perseverance Calvin concludes: 'From this we infer that they [believers] are out of danger of falling away because the Son of God, asking that their godliness be kept constant, did not suffer a refusal. What did Christ wish to have us learn from this but to trust that we shall ever remain safe because we have been made his once for all?' (III.24.6)

Assurance of the future salvation is based solely on the fact that Christ cares about us. We ourselves are unable to keep our own faith and left to ourselves we would certainly perish. God 'must establish us and strengthen our faith by giving us an invincible perseverance to hold out to the end' (*Sermons on Ephesians* 72). But since it is Christ who keeps us we cannot fail to attain perfection. Thus assurance of ultimate salvation is not presumption or 'overassurance' (III.24.6) but 'simple confidence' (III.24.7) in Christ.

> Therefore when we have our adoption engraven in our hearts then... we have a good and infallible pledge that God will guide us unto the end, and that since he has begun to lead us into the way of salvation, he will bring us to the perfection to which he calls us, because, in truth, without him we could not continue so much as a single day (*Sermons on Ephesians* 48).

'The end' of our salvation should be understood in terms of resurrection and eternal heavenly life. Calvin recognizes the fact that resurrection may seem unthinkable and impossible but he says that resurrection of Christ and omnipotence of God should strengthen our faith. 'It is difficult to believe that bodies, when consumed with rottenness, will at length be raised up in their season... Scripture provides two helps by which faith may overcome this great obstacle: one in the parallel of Christ's resurrection; the other in the omnipotence of God' (III. 25.3).

Karl Barth's Doubts about John Calvin's Assurance

True to himself Calvin expounds the doctrine of resurrection in terms of our union with Christ:

> Now whenever we consider the resurrection, let Christ's image come before us. In the nature which he took from us he so completed the course of mortal life that now, having obtained immortality, he is the pledge of our coming resurrection... And to separate him from ourselves is not permissible and not even possible, without tearing him apart. From this, Paul argues: "If the dead do not rise up again, then Christ did not rise up again". For he takes it as an agreed principle that it was not for himself alone that Christ was subjected to death, or that he obtained victory over death by rising again. Rather there was begun in the Head what must be completed in all members... (III.25.3)

Consideration of God's omnipotence is another way in which we may strengthen our faith in resurrection:

> But let us remember that no one is truly persuaded of the coming resurrection unless he is seized with wonder, and ascribes to the power of God its due glory. Isaiah lifted up by this assurance, exclaims: 'Thy dead men shall live; my body shall rise. O dwellers in the dust, awake and praise'. In desperate circumstances David raises himself to God, the Author of life, to whom 'belongs the escape from death', as it is said in the psalm. Job also, more like a corpse than a man, relying on God's might, doubts not that he will arise as a whole man at that day: 'I know my redeemer lives, and in the Last Day he will arise upon the dust and I shall again be covered with my skin and in my flesh I shall see God; I myself shall see, and not another' (III.25.4).

Apparently Calvin understands the passages which he quoted from the Old Testament literally. For him resurrection is continuation of human life in body. Of course, the life is heavenly and the body is glorified but still it is human life and human body. Our souls are immortal but it is only a part of the truth. The human souls will live forever in the same bodies in which they were clothed on earth and which God will resurrect. Calvin denies the idea that the resurrected bodies will be essentially different from bodies which we now have. 'Equally monstrous is the error of those who imagine that the souls will not receive the same bodies with which they are now clothed but will be furnished with new and different ones' (III.25.7). Calvin unfolds the biblical teaching about resurrection in a very clear and convincing manner. On the one hand, he refers to a number of passages in which human body is honored: apostle Paul prays for keeping our souls and bodies sound, body is the temple of God, we are members of Christ, we pray with lifted hands, and are called to offer our bodies as a living sacrifice etc. On the other hand, he quotes a number of biblical texts which plainly speak about resurrection of our present bodies. For example, he points to what Paul says in 1 Cor. 15:53:

> Nor does Scripture define anything more clearly than the resurrection of the flesh that we now bear. "For this perishable nature," says Paul, "must put on the imperishable, and this mortal nature must put on immortality." If God made new bodies, where would this change of quality appear? If Scripture had said that we must be renewed, an ambiguous expression would perhaps have given occasion for their cavil. Now when, pointing at the bodies that encompass us, he promises them incorruption, he is openly enough denying that new ones are made (III.25.7.).

After commenting on other passages from both Testaments he comes back to our union with Christ: we should not and cannot tear apart redemptive work of Christ and separate His death and resurrection. Christ bore our sin on the cross in his body, and he was raised from the dead in his body. This is the foundation of our belief in eternal life and hope for the future blessedness: 'We must hold fast to that fellowship which the apostle proclaims: that we arise because Christ arose. For nothing is less likely than that our flesh, in which we bear about the death of Christ himself, should be deprived of Christ's resurrection' (III.25.7).

Beyond the Formal Definition: Assurance Coexists with Doubt

Doubt

Calvin admits that the true believers at times 'not only feel disquietude, but sometimes tremble, overcome with terror' (III.2.17).

Karl Barth's Doubts about John Calvin's Assurance

> When we say that faith must be certain and secure, we certainly speak not of an assurance which is never affected by doubt, nor a security which anxiety never assails, we rather maintain that believers have a perpetual struggle with their own distrust, and are thus far from thinking that their consciences possess a placid quiet, uninterrupted by perturbation (III.2.17).

Does Calvin contradict himself? What does he mean when he says that true faith is 'sure and firm knowledge' and then adds that the believer can be 'overcome with terror'? Edward Dowey suggests that in order to understand Calvin's thought we must look beyond his formal definition of faith and set it in the full context of his theology:

> Calvin is a better psychologist of faith than any of the elements of his teaching as represented by the terms of the formal definition would lead us to believe. When Calvin defined faith as a "steady and certain knowledge," he was describing it essentially and therefore normatively. He was conscious that these two words do not give an adequate phenomenology of believing (193).

So let us look beyond and see that Calvin believed that doubt co-exists with assurance and that for him this co-existence is not so much a theoretical paradox as an experiential reality.

Doubt wages war against assurance but never expels it from the heart. 'On the other hand, whatever be the mode in which they are assailed, we deny that they fall off and abandon that sure confidence which they have formed in the mercy of God' (Dowey 193). For Calvin, doubt in the believer is not the same as absence of assurance. Beeke also recognizes this fact: 'Even as the believer is tormented with fleshly doubts, his spirit trusts God's mercy...' (48). Co-existence of doubt and assurance may be well illustrated from the life of David. David had faith but he also had great doubts at times (Pss. 42:6; 31:22; 77:9; 116:7). 'And yet amid those commotions, faith sustains the believer's heart... thus David, when he seemed to be overwhelmed, ceased not by urging himself forward to ascend to God' (III.2.17). Not only the triumph of faith over doubt but also the very struggle itself shows that the believer does not loose certainty of God's favor when doubt comes: what would fight doubt if assurance were absent? Doubt is present in the believer as in a person who already has assurance. The believer does not strive to attain assurance, he fights to preserve it.

That doubt does not expel assurance from the heart of the believer is also evident from the opposite case of the wicked king Ahaz (cf. Is. 7). There is no struggle in him. When doubt comes he gives up his hypocritical trust in God and seeks other ways apart from God to protect himself from the foreign invasion. He never had real faith therefore doubt encounters no resistance in him and does not have to conquer his assurance. Beeke confirms our analysis of Calvin's thought: 'The reprobate do not have this struggle for they neither love God nor hate sin' (48).

David's faith is his fortress, while doubt is the enemy who assails it. When the enemy comes David defends his fortress and his fortress defends him; he struggles and he triumphs. 'Though we are distracted by various thoughts, it does not follow that we are immediately divested of faith' (III.2.18). Ahaz has no fortress, when the enemy comes he has nothing to defend and he is defended by nothing; he does not struggle, he simply gives up to the enemy. '...[W]e again maintain, that faith remaining fixed in the believer's breast never can be eradicated from it... unbelief reigns not in the heart of believers, but only assails them from without' (III.2.21). Doubt is present in the unbeliever in a different manner: it is the owner of the heart in which assurance has never dwelt.

> The fact that the believer prays proves that he always has assurance. How could he pray if he was not sure that he may call God his father? Assurance is absolutely necessary for a sincere prayer and prayer is the evidence that the believer has not lost assurance. The papists say that we must doubt it [assurance] and that we can come to God only with a hope that he will receive us; but to assure ourselves of it – that we ought not to do, for that would be too great a presumption. But when we pray to God, we must call him Father, at least if we are the scholars of our Lord Jesus Christ, for he has taught us to do so. Now, is it at a venture that we call him Father, or are we sure of it in ourselves that he is our Father? If not, then there would be nothing by hypocrisy in our prayers, and the first word that we utter would be a lie. The

papists then never know what it is to pray to God, seeing that they cannot be assured of their salvation.

> But... the Scripture shows that to pray to God rightly, we must have belief in Jesus Christ, which gives us confidence, and upon that confidence we by and by conceive boldness. Be that as it may, we must not be hesitant nor yet doubt, but we must be thoroughly resolved and persuaded in ourselves that God counts us as his children (*Sermons on Ephesians* 28-29).

In passing it is interesting to note that there is, indeed, no alternative definition of faith with which we could replace Calvin's 'sure and firm knowledge'. Calvin himself affirms this when he asks whether we should think 'that faith consists not of a sure and clear, but only of an obscure and confused, understanding of the divine will in regard to us?' (III.2.18) His answer to the question ('By no means') shows that he cannot conceive of an alternative.

Calvin regards assurance as inseparable from faith: 'As soon as the minutest particle of faith is instilled into our minds, we begin to behold the face of God placid, serene, and propitious' (III.2.19). If we have just a particle of faith and at the same time have assurance in God's favor to us then we conclude that faith and assurance are inseparable. As soon as we have faith we also have assurance; to have faith is to see the peaceful face of God, which is the same as to be assured of one's own salvation. Faith is always accompanied by assurance. And as we already saw, from the very definition of faith, assurance not only always accompanies faith but actually is essential part of it: '...firm and stable constancy of heart... is the chief part of faith' (III.2.33).

Both faith and assurance can grow. To have a particle of faith is like seeing sunlight from a tiny prison cell (III.2.19). To grow in faith is to enlarge the window through which light comes to us. We see first less and then more light, but we see nothing else but light. The sure knowledge of the first particle of faith is nothing else but sure knowledge. Its nature does not change though its fullness increases as we learn more about Christ's promises to us (III.2.19). Therefore, if we have assurance only when we have full knowledge of God's promise in Christ than we can never attain assurance at all because we are 'constantly engaged in learning' and 'a subject

John Calvin

which is of boundless extent cannot be comprehended by our feeble and narrow capacities' (III.2.20).

The source of doubt in the believer is twofold: ignorance and temptation. Ignorance has already been discussed. Temptations come from circumstances and conscience. 'Therefore, whether adverse circumstances betoken the wrath of God, or conscience finds the subject and matter within itself, unbelief thence draws weapons and engines to put faith to flight… To withstand these assaults, faith, arms and fortifies itself with the word of God' (III.2.21).

The relation between doubt and assurance can be summed up in the following diagrams. The first represents the false notion: as if doubt and assurance cannot co-exist in one person simultaneously. The second shows that assurance is intrinsic for the believer while doubt comes from without. The arrows between doubt and assurance show that they are in conflict; the double arrows underscore that assurance ultimately wins. The dotted arrows indicate sources of doubt and assurance.

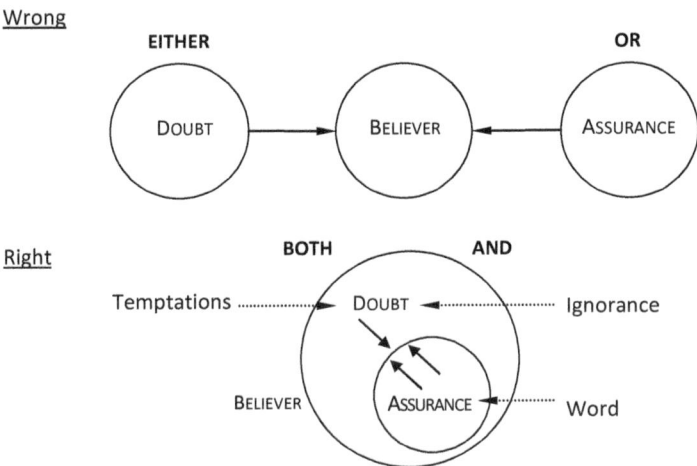

Thus we see that for Calvin the reality of doubts in the believer's experience does not disprove his thesis that assurance is part of faith and that the believer always has assurance, and never loses it.

Karl Barth's Doubts about John Calvin's Assurance

Fear

Fear is another reality of believer's emotional experience. Fear of God seems incompatible with assurance of his favor. How can we come boldly to God if we fear him? However fear 'so far from impairing the security of faith, tends rather to establish it' (III.2.22). Examples of divine vengeance on ungodly alert the believer to his own sinfulness, considerations of his wickedness drive him to rely more on God and distrust his own strength. When the believer is reminded by the beacons from the past that his wickedness deserves God's punishment he clings to God in order to escape his wrath. When Paul exhorts Corinthians 'Let him that thinks he stands take heed lest he fall', 'he does not bid us waver, as if we had no security for our steadfastness: he only removes arrogance and rash confidence in our strength' (III.2.23). 'Then, when he bids us to work out our salvation with fear and trembling, all he requires is, that we accustom ourselves to think very meanly of our own strength, and confide in the strength of the Lord' (III.2.23). Fear does not destroy confidence in God but confidence in man himself. Fear 'shakes off carnal torpor which suppresses faith' (III.2.22).

At this point Calvin considers an objection to the possibility of assurance related to the problem of fear. Objection: We cannot always have assurance but we constantly move between hope and fear because 'if you look to Christ salvation is certain; if you return to yourself damnation is certain'. God offers us salvation, in Christ but we are unworthy to receive it.

Answer. It is true that 'if you look to yourself damnation is certain'. But 'His righteousness covers your sins – his salvation extinguishes your condemnation; he interposes with his worthiness, and so prevents your unworthiness from coming into the view of God' (III.2.24). We are united to Christ, 'it will never do to separate Christ from us', therefore we should not worry about our unworthiness. In other words, it is true that we are unworthy to receive salvation from God, but we receive it because we are united to Christ and on this basis we can have assurance. Our unworthiness does not take away our assurance because the former is counteracted by union with Christ.

Calvin upholds the difference between servile fear and 'voluntary fear which becomes sons' (III.2.27). To have servile fear is to fear God only because of punishment. Unbelievers knows of no other relationship with God but only of that of Judge and criminal. Therefore he cannot approach God boldly. He fears his punishment. To have fear of a son is to fear God not so much because of possible punishment but primarily because God is a good Father. 'He who considers with himself what kind of a father God is to us, will see sufficient reason, even were there no hell, why the thought of offending him should seem more dreadful than any death' (III.2.26). Believer's fear is not fear of hell but fear of insulting the One who loves him so much.

However Calvin is very realistic about our tendency to sin and admits that fear of punishment should not be completely cast away, it can have secondary place. 'But so prone is our carnal nature to indulgence in sin, that, in order to curb it in every way, we must also give place to the thought that all iniquity is abomination to the Master under whom we live; that those who, by wicked lives, provoke his anger, will not escape his vengeance' (III.2.27).

Fear, like doubt, is a reality of believer's experience. Paradoxically fear, far from destroying assurance, strengthens it by forcing us to abandon self-reliance and rely more on God and inhibition of sin. Therefore, we come to the same conclusion with respect to fear as we have come in respect of doubts, namely, that it does not expel assurance. Due consideration of divine wrath and loving care leads to more confidence in God and inhibits sin.

Peace
In light of what has just been said about the work of the Holy Spirit in our minds and hearts, we can understand biblical teaching about peace which the believer possesses. On the one hand 'the minds of believers are seldom at rest', on the other hand David

experienced 'delightful tranquility'. As doubt co-exists with assurance so anxiety co-exists with peace.

The former paradox has been discussed at length and resolved above, the latter may be solved in the following words: 'Not that David was uniformly in this joyful frame; but in so far as the measure of his faith made him sensible of the divine favor, he glories in intrepidly despising everything that could disturb his peace of mind' (III.2.37). As in the case of doubt which encounters the resistance of assurance and is defeated by it, so anxiety meets opposition of peace and is conquered too. Anxiety comes to the believer as a person who already possesses peace. Peace fights for itself and never really leaves the believer.

Hope

We hope for the things which we do not see, and faith functions as a support of our hope. This is one of the ways Calvin understands the definition of faith given in Hebrews 1:11. However he prefers another interpretation of this passage. The things we hope for are incomprehensible for reason alone, we can know them only as far as we believe God's word about them. '[T]he things pertaining to our salvation are too high to be perceived by our senses, or seen by our eyes, or handled by our hands… We contemplate them only in his word, of the truth of which we ought to be so persuaded that we should count whatever he speaks as already done and fulfilled' (III.2.41). On this interpretation hope is a fruit of faith: we hope for the things which we do not possess and do not really understand but of which we have sure knowledge by faith. We could not hope for them if we did not have faith. We have knowledge of them by faith therefore we expect them.

> Wherever this faith is alive, it must have along with it the hope of eternal salvation as its inseparable companion. Or rather, it engenders and brings forth hope from itself. For if faith, as has been said above, is a sure persuasion of the truth of God – that it can neither lie to us, nor deceive us, nor become void – then those who have grasped this certainty assuredly expect the time to come

when God will fulfill his promises, which they are persuaded cannot but be true (III.2.42).

Such understanding of the nature of hope leads Calvin to define hope in terms of faith: '[H]ope is nothing else than expectation of those things which faith has believed to have been truly promised by God' (III.2.42). Thus hope is not understandable apart from faith because the former is the result of the latter. Moreover it is a necessary result: 'When this hope is taken away, however eloquently or elegantly we discourse concerning faith, we are convinced of having none' (III.2.42).

The relationship between faith and hope is a reciprocal one: 'Faith is the foundation upon which hope rests, hope nourishes and sustains faith' (III.2.42). 'Hope sustains faith to the final goal, that it may not fail in middle-course, or even at the starting gate'. Why does faith fail? There is a number of reasons. 'First, the Lord by deferring his promises often holds our minds in suspense longer than we would wish... Occasionally he not only allows us to faint but exhibits open indignation toward us... Scoffers also rise up...' (III.2.42). Therefore 'we must keep our faith buttressed by patient hope' (III.2.42).

Conclusion

'[T]he certainty of which Calvin has made so much does not in fact issue in psychological serenity... Certainty is never "carnal security", but an active, existential, struggling certainty' (Dowey 194, 197). Thus the full psychological portrait of the true believer according to Calvin looks like this:

Karl Barth's Doubts about John Calvin's Assurance

Faith-assurance is put into the inner circle because it belongs to the very nature of a person as a believer. It never leaves him. Only he who possesses it can be called a true believer. Doubt, anxiety, fear, on the contrary, are put into the outer circle because they are always external to the believer. They may be present as foreign elements in him but they never influence the believer's life as faith-assurance does. 'Doubts may be outwardly, but never inwardly, predominant, for Christ dwells in us' (Dowey 198). Finally, hope and peace are next to faith-assurance because they are the fruits of the latter.

At the end of the day Calvin could perhaps agree with these words of Dowey: 'If the bare words of his definition of faith make it "steady and certain knowledge", according to Calvin, we must notice that such faith is never realized. We could formulate a description of existing faith for him as a "steady and certain knowledge invariably attacked by vicious doubts and fears over which it is finally victorious"' (197).

2. KARL BARTH

Approach

Like John Calvin, Karl Barth (1886-1968) does not treat the doctrine of assurance separately as an independent part of theological system. In Calvin's system assurance was included in faith. To understand Calvin's doctrine of assurance we had to expound his doctrine of faith. The same may be said about Barth, only in his case the doctrine of assurance is a subtopic of the doctrine of election. This fact determines our approach to exposition of Barth's teaching on assurance. First, we will outline his understanding of election. Second, we will tackle the issue of universalism. Third, we will present his own doctrine of assurance as the corollary of the doctrine of election.

However we cannot stop at this point and must take one more step. Fourth, we have to put Barth's doctrine of assurance in the broader context of his theology. Barth's usage of language may create a problem for the students of his thought. He constantly used traditional orthodox terminology but gave it different meanings. Therefore we risk misunderstanding Barth's doctrine of assurance completely if we neglect the study of such concepts as sin, faith, reconciliation, and eternal life in his thought. Unfortunately, because of different kinds of limitations, we could not analyze these concepts on the basis of primary sources but used information from secondary ones. This procedure is, of course, far from adequate but choosing between two evils, namely, leaving the doctrine of assurance lonely and naked, and elucidating it by means of secondary sources, we have chosen what from our point of view was the lesser evil.

Karl Barth's Doubts about John Calvin's Assurance Doctrine of Election

Points of contact and divergence

For Barth the doctrine of election is anything but unimportant in Christian theology. It is not of secondary or even of primary importance. It is more. It is the Gospel itself. 'And we introduce the first and most radical point with our thesis that the doctrine of election must be understood quite definitely and unequivocally as Gospel... The election of grace is the sum of the Gospel – we must put it as pointedly as that. But more, the election of grace is the whole of the Gospel, the Gospel *in nuce*. It is the very essence of all good news' (*Church Dogmatics, II/2* 13-14)[3]. In the course of the exposition of the doctrine of election, Barth makes it quite clear why he makes such an unusual statement. This bold statement may appall those among us who think that the doctrine of election belongs to the sphere of abstract theologizing and who can hardly imagine how it is possible to make the doctrine of election the center of the gospel preaching. However, already at this point in *Church Dogmatics*, Barth hints at the source of his boldness: 'That God wills neither to be without the world nor against it can never be stated more clearly or forcibly than when we speak of His election... of and from himself God has decided for this loftiest and most radical movement towards His creation, ordaining and constituting himself its Friend and Benefactor' (26).

All serious statements about election, says Barth, have three things in common. They uphold freedom, mystery, and righteousness of divine predestination.

Freedom of election means that God's decision is independent of all creaturely decisions (19). Grace cannot be constrained by any merit, 'nor can it be held up or rendered nugatory' by the creature (19), therefore there is no place for self-glorying. Since God in his grace 'unconditionally precedes the creature' (27) the freedom of election implies 'the final and severest humiliation of the creature' (28). However humiliation does not mean despair: 'Where God does not despair, the creature cannot

---
[3] In this chapter almost all quotations of Barth are taken from *Church Dogmatics*, II/2. For the sake of brevity we will indicate only page numbers below when we quote from this source.

despair' (29). It even can be said that 'humiliation is really and in the same moment exaltation' (29), because 'grace is the Nevertheless of the divine love to the creature' (28). Finally, freedom of God's election means that the object of election himself becomes free. On the one hand he is free from accusation, curse and bondage of sin as well as from death which is the result of sin, on the other he is free for thankfulness, service, and joy (30).

There is a certain mystery in election (although as we will see later Barth's understanding of this mystery is quite different from the traditional one). Election is 'the divine resolve and decree whose basis is hidden and inscrutable... The will of God knows no Wherefore? It is an absolute Therefore, the ultimate Therefore of all' (20). In face of this mystery the creature must be silent for the sake of hearing and for the sake of obedience (30). This mystery 'disturbs us but does not disquiet us' (31). It leads us to rest from anxiety as to how can God say ultimate Yes to fallen creature (31). The mystery of election, rightly understood, gives us peace and causes us to wonder, taking away anxiety and self-despair (32).

Righteousness of election means that God exercises judgment on the creature, maintains His own worth and makes us aware of our own limitations (33). 'The righteousness of God utterly crushes us' (33). But it is only one side of the truth. It is also true that God blesses is us by his righteousness. 'The righteousness of God in his election means, then, that as a righteous Judge God perceives and estimates as such the lost case of the creature, and that in spite of its opposition He gives sentence in its favour, fashioning for it His own righteousness' (34). Later Barth works out the idea that God fashions for creature His own righteousness Christologically and consistently develops the Pauline insight which he himself expresses in the following words: 'It [righteousness of God] lifts accusation from us and yet it does not expose God himself to accusation' (34).

Leaving the introductory remarks about Barth's doctrine of election which showed that his teaching is innovative but is not completely detached from the traditional formulations we must now turn to the fundamental Christological statement which fully determines the main features of his doctrine of election.

Jesus Christ, Electing God and Elected Man

The origin of the doctrine of election may be explained in a number of ways. We may mention two of them which lead Barth to his main statement about election. One the hand we have those theologians who seek to answer the question why some men believe in the gospel and some do not, e.g. Augustine (39). The doctrine of election gives an apparently straightforward answer: those who believe have been chosen by God, and vice versa. On the other hand, in the history of theology, the doctrine of election often became a part of the doctrine of providence and election was considered as a particular case of more general concept of providence, e.g. Aquinas (45). Both approaches are inadequate for the same reason: they consider election in abstract (49) while it should be considered concretely. They fail to base the doctrine of election in the self-revelation of God which is Jesus Christ. 'If we would know who God is, and what is the meaning and purpose of His election, and in what respect he is the electing God, then we must look away from all others, and excluding all side-glances or secondary thoughts, we must look only upon and to the name of Jesus Christ, and the existence and history of the people of God enclosed in Him' (54).

However these two approaches 'do contain decisive moments of truth... If their incorrect form is ignored, and they are taken together, the two answers just mentioned and rejected do have the merit of indicating the real problem of the doctrine: God as the subject of election and man as its object' (52). 'The real problem' must be solved Christologically, and not on the basis of a general view of man and a general concept of God. 'It is the name of Jesus Christ which, according to the divine self-revelation, forms the focus at which the two decisive beams of the truth forced upon us converge and unite: on the one hand the electing God and on the other elected man' (59).

In its simplest and most comprehensive form the dogma of predestination consists, then, in the assertion that the divine predestination is the election of

Jesus Christ. But the concept of election has s double reference – to the elector and to the elected. And so, too, the name of Jesus Christ has within itself the double reference: the One called by this name is both very God and very man. Thus the simplest form of the dogma may be divided at once into the two assertions that Jesus Christ is the electing God, and that He is also elected man (103).

First, Jesus Christ is the electing God. This assertion is a polemic against the traditional idea of *decretum absolutum* (103). Traditionally, it is believed that God made decision in eternity and its basis is wholly hidden from us (103). Why and how God made the choice he did we cannot ask, let alone know. Calvinists say that God's decision is based on grounds which are just and adequate although beyond our comprehension. Lutherans try to comfort us stating that this decision is determined by the general loving-kindness of God toward us (110). In either case there can be no assurance of election because the electing God is unknown to us (111). In quest of assurance those who hold to traditional doctrine of *decretum absolutum* will inevitably find the basis of assurance either in 'a pretended knowledge of the secret of divine decree' or 'certain works of faith whose existence is supposed to give direct confirmation of faith and indirect confirmation of election' (113). However when the place of the absolute decree is taken by Jesus Christ all uncertainty of election disappears (104). 'We must not ask concerning any other but Him. In no depth of the Godhead shall we encounter any other but Him... There is no such thing as a *decretum absolutum*. There is no such thing as a will of God apart from the will of Jesus Christ... Jesus Christ reveals to us our election as an election which is made by Him, by His will which is also the will of God. He tells us that He Himself is the One who elects us... As we believe in Him and hear His Word and hold fast by His decision, we can know with a certainty which nothing can ever shake that we are the elect of God' (115).

Second, Jesus Christ is the elected man. Apparently, Barth states what orthodox theologians always believed on the basis of such passages as 1 Peter 1:20. Jesus Christ was chosen by God to be the means of our salvation. However, Barth, although he does not exclude the orthodox understanding, means something quite new and different when he says that Jesus Christ is electing God. This statement actually changes the object of election: it denies that the posterity of Adam is the object of election and asserts that the proper object is the man Jesus Christ.

> It tells us that before all created reality, before all being and becoming in time, before time itself, in the pre-temporal eternity of God, the eternal divine decision as such has as its object and content the existence of this one created being, the man Jesus of Nazareth, and the work of this man in His life and death, His humiliation and exaltation, His obedience and merit. It tells us further that in and with the existence of this man the eternal divine decision has as its object and content the execution of the divine covenant with man, the salvation of all men. In this function this man is the object of the eternal divine decision and foreordination (116).

Men as such are not the objects of divine election. Their election is secondary, they are elected in Him. 'His election is the original and all-inclusive election; the election which absolutely unique, but which in this very uniqueness is universally meaningful and efficacious, because it is the election of Him who himself elects' (117).

Election to Suffering

In this section we come to the most beautiful part of Barth's theology. It is beautiful in the language used, in the ideas expressed, and in the emotions contained in it. It may be doubted how orthodox the meaning of his statements is but it cannot be denied that their form is one of the best ways to express the central Christian idea: the cross of Christ. Each time Barth touches this theme he creates a literary masterpiece and for this if for nothing else his posterity should be grateful to him. Moreover this theme is of crucial importance for evaluating Barth's universalism.

God's wrath is kindled against men. It is not the creatureliness of men which causes God's wrath but the abuse of its creatureliness (123). The distinction is important: it is not the infinite qualitative gap between God and creation which makes men guilty and deserving God's judgment but their sinfulness. 'In himself and such man will always do as Adam did in Genesis 3. And for this reason, according to the will and counsel of God, man in himself and as such incurs the rejection which rests upon his temptation and corruption' (122). The good news of election is that in Christmas message 'The Word became flesh' we already have the message of Good Friday (122). 'The election of man Jesus means, then, that a wrath is kindled, a sentence is pronounced and finally executed, a rejection is actualized' (122).

The election of Jesus Christ to suffering means nothing less than His substitutionary suffering for men culminating in violent death on the cross. The righteousness of God does not know another way of reconciliation than punishing sin in the person of Jesus Christ. 'The rejection which all men incurred, the wrath of God under which all men lie, the death which all men must die, God in His love for men transfers from all eternity to Him in whom He loves and elects them, and whom He elects at their head and in their place. God from all eternity ordains this obedient One in order that He might bear the suffering which the disobedient have deserved and which for the sake of God's righteousness must necessarily be born' (123).

The suffering to which Jesus Christ is elected does not consist only of being a creature and living in the human world. The suffering of the elect Man whatever they may be during his earthly life end with suffering on the cross, which is not natural but caused by wrath of God. This suffering may be described as judgment and penalty. 'But it means that God must and will reject man as he is in himself. And he does so. But he does it in the person of the elected man Jesus. And in him He loves man as he is in himself. He elects Jesus, then, at the head and in the place of others. The wrath of God the judgment and the penalty, fall, then, upon Him' (124). 'For all those, then, whom God elects in His Son, the essence of the free grace of God consists in the fact that in this same Jesus God who is the Judge takes the place of the judged, and they are fully acquitted, therefore, from sin and its guilt and penalty' (125).

Barth returns again and again to this idea that election of Jesus Christ means rejection of Him for our sakes. For instance, when he discusses the idea of double predestination – election implies rejection – he readily accepts this teaching but as may be expected, reinterprets it Christologically. The elected and the rejected man is Jesus Christ. And rejection of Jesus is not something which happens in the mind of God but it takes place on the plane of history.

Barth starts the discussion of *praedestinatio gemina* with intriguing statement: 'It is obvious that when we confess that God has elected fellowship with man for Himself we are stating one thing, and when we confess that God has elected fellowship with Himself for man we are stating quite another' (162). At first glance, the distinction which Barth makes here begs a question: is not the fellowship between God and man mutual? But as he proceeds to develop this thought he gives clear answer to this question. And here we quote from Barth at length otherwise we may break the chain of thought and miss the beauty of the language:

> It is one thing for God to elect and predestinate Himself to fellowship with man, and quite another for God to predestinate man to fellowship with Himself. Both are God's self-giving to man. But if the latter means unequivocally that a gift is made to man, the former certainly does not mean that God gives or procures Himself anything – for what could God give or procure Himself in giving to man a share in His own being? What we have to consider under this aspect is simply God's hazarding of his Godhead and power and status. For man it means an infinite gain, an unheard of advancement, that God should give Himself to him as his own possession, that God should be his God. But for God it means inevitably a certain compromising of Himself that He should determine to enter into this covenant. Where man stands only to gain, God stands only to lose. And because the eternal divine predestination is identical with the election of Jesus Christ, its twofold content is that God wills to lose in order that man may gain. There is a sure and certain salvation for man, and sure and certain risk for God (162).

At this point we want to repeat that Barth makes an important distinction between man as a good creature and as a fallen one. Electing fellowship with man for Himself God risked twice. The man even as the good creation lives on the edge of an abyss therefore he may fail to do God's will. 'The very fact that man was not God but creature, even though he was a good creature, had meant already a certain jeopardizing of the honour of God as whose instrument man had been created. Would this good instrument extol God's honor as was meet, as God himself extolled it, as a good instrument ought to extol it?' (163). The risk taken by God was actually far greater because man crossed the frontier of impossible and fell. 'But the man with whom the eternal will of God has to do is not this man; or rather, it is this man, not good as God created him, but fallen away from God. In fact, then the risk taken by God was far greater. His partner in this covenant is not man on the brink of danger but man already overtaken by it' (164).

The idea of twofold risk as clearly as possible expresses the idea that the wrath of God and rejection of man are not the result of what may be called 'ontological guilt', as if men deserve God's wrath just because they are men and God. The judgment which God pronounces over men has moral character: men deserve rejection not for their creatureliness but for failing to do the will of God and extol the honour of God. Sin which causes rejection of man is not ontological but moral. Thus the suspicion which may arise from reading early writings of Barth (such as *Romans*) that God's judgment over men is caused by their creaturely limitations is dispelled by what Barth says in this volume of *Church Dogmatics*.

We may conclude the discussion of election to suffering with these words of Barth:

> If we would know what it was that God elected for himself when He elected fellowship with man, then we can answer only that he elected our rejection. He made it His own. He bore it and suffered it with all its most bitter consequences. For the sake of this choice and for the sake of man He hazarded Himself wholly and utterly... Judas who betrays Him He elects as an apostle. The sentence of Pilate He elects as a revelation of His judgment on the world. He elect the cross of Golgotha as His kingly throne. He elects the tomb in the garden as the scene of His being as the living God. That is how God loved the world (164-165).

Karl Barth's Doubts about John Calvin's Assurance

Purified Supralapsarianism

To sum up Barth's doctrine of election and at the same time to point out the most important differences between Barth and orthodoxy we may describe Barth's doctrine as 'purified supralapsarianism'. Barth himself uses this expression (142) to indicate that he both stands in the tradition of the classical supralapsarianism and significantly advances beyond traditional teaching.

Barth is the heir of the 'supra' scheme of decrees in that sense that he regards the decree of election as foundational and preceding all other decrees and activities of God *ad extra*. 'The primal and basic purpose of the eternal counsel of this God in relation to the world is to impart and reveal Himself – and with Himself His glory, He Himself being the very essence of glory. And because all things are His creation, because He is the Lord of all things, this primal and basic purpose is the beginning of all things, the eternal reality in which everything future is already determined and comprehended' (140).

However Barth distances himself from the orthodox position on four points importance of which for Barth's doctrine of election is impossible to overemphasize. They explain in what way Barth purified Supralapsarianism. Therefore we will pay very close attention to what Barth has to say about the object of election, the fixed character of the divine decree, the equilibrium between election and rejection, and the absolute decree.

First, the object of election. Barth states the orthodox position: 'Supralapsarians, Infralapsarians and mediators all agree that the controverted *obiectum praedestinationis*, elected or rejected man, must be identified directly and independently with the partly elected and partly rejected individual descendants of Adam, both in the mass and also in detail' (133). Over against this position Barth presents his own idea: 'He [God] wills man: not the idea of man, not humanity, not human individuals in the mass or in particular; or rather all these, but *in concreto* and not *in abstracto*. He wills man, His man, elected man, man predestined as the witness to his glory and the object of his love. In this man, but only in him, He wills humanity and every individual man and what we may describe as the idea of humanity. But first and specifically and immediately He wills man, His man, man elected by Him' (140-141). Obviously, this man is Jesus Christ. From this first point which radically distinguishes Barth from the Reformed tradition flow other three as its corollaries.

Second, the fixed character of the divine decree. The traditional position according to Barth is this: '...in God's eternal decree predestination (an therefore the election or rejection of individuals) implies the setting up of a fixed system which the temporal life and history of individuals can only fulfill and affirm' (134). This understanding, argues Barth, originated in the attempt to distinguish between human and divine decrees. The former is changeable because the lawgiver, however great tyrant he may be is, a living being whose will changes. The latter, therefore must be unchangeable, since the will of God does not change: '...all thought of an alteration or suspension of the [divine] decree is excluded' (181). Thus, God's eternal election 'is not an action, an electing and deciding, which is still continued in time. God's living action in the present consists only in the execution of this decree, the fulfillment of an election and decision already made... His speech and activity in the temporal present are only an echo of the note which was struck in His eternal decree' (181). Barth uses the image of a letter to underscore how unacceptable for him the orthodox idea of fixed decision: 'God did predestinate. In time He predestinates no longer... That which was in the beginning with God is an authoritative and all-powerful letter... After that first and all-embracing act of life, God Himself, the living God, retired behind this letter... He delivered up the creaturely life to the rule of this letter' (182). From Barth's point of view such understanding comes close to Deism and even atheism.

For Barth, God is a living God, therefore his decree must be living and not dead, 'a decree that is infinitely more living than any decree of man' (183). The election certainly happened in the eternal past, but it also is happening in the present and will happen in the future. God continues to makes decision 'at every moment of time' (183). The music of election does not belong just to the past. 'God is never an echo. He is and continues to be and always will be an independent note or sound' (183). 'Predestination is the divine act of will itself and not an abstraction from or fixed and static result of it' (181).

The living character of decree, or to put it in other words the fact that election is an event, 'unchanged and unchangeably the history, encounter and decision between God and man', this fact implies that we may and should expect from God 'new decisions in time' (186). 'As the Bible itself presents the matter, there is no election which cannot be followed by rejection, no rejection which cannot be followed by election... And since His life is the dynamic of that order, developments and alterations in it are always possible and do in fact take place' (186-187).

Barth perceives how dangerous this thesis may be and what undesired development it may be given. The problem is that in the traditional framework the destiny of man must be decided by someone: either by God or by man himself. A dilemma arises. One horn of the dilemma is this. If the destiny of man is not fixed and it depends on the sovereign will of God than we arrive at the scholastic notion of *potential absoluta*. In other words, we are involved in horrible game: '...a mere game which god plays with man, a game which is completely bewildering in its hiddenness and unexpectedness. And in this game of judgment and mercy, what chance is there, if any, of a final knowledge of how one stands with God?' (190) The other horn of dilemma is the following. If the destiny of man is not fixed and depends on the decision of man than we arrive at Pelagianism or at best at Lutheran synergism. The freedom of God's election is lost, it becomes dependent on man's will.

As may be expected the dilemma cannot be solved in the traditional framework and Barth's Christological innovation must come to our help. 'If predestination is identical with election of Jesus Christ, there can be no question of any confusion between God's living predestinating, deciding and electing, and the vacillation of a *potentia absoluta* or a game capriciously played by the Deity with its creatures' (192). Certainly there is nothing unsure or unstable about election of Jesus Christ. He is the elected man and all particular individuals are elected in Him. The eternal will of God is clearly revealed in Jesus Christ. Then, 'if predestination is identified with the election of Jesus Christ, it follows, secondly, that there can be no question of a limiting and conditioning of the freedom of God in which this decision is made by the mystery of the existentiality of a complementary human decision' (193). Even less it can be doubted that election of Jesus Christ is dependent on any man's will and decision!

Formally, the dilemma is solved if in accordance with Barth's innovation we change the object of election from men to the man. However, the dilemma is solved not only formally but also materially as will become clear in discussion of the remaining two points which distinguish Barth's supralapsarianism from the traditional one.

Third, equilibrium between election and rejection. Traditionally it is believed that 'when God set up this fixed system which anticipated the life-history and destiny of every individual as such, then in the same way, in the same sense, with the same emphasis, and in exact equilibrium in every respect, God uttered both a Yes and a No, accepting some and rejecting others' (134).

Here we come again to the teaching about double predestination. As we have already seen Barth accepts the terminology of double predestination, he accepts the idea that election implies rejection and that God not only elects but also rejects. And again Barth reinterprets this Christologically and his idea of election to suffering begins to play an all important role at this crucial point. God, of course, says a Yes and a No but they are directed to men only in the election of Jesus Christ. Jesus Christ is the object of divine Yes and No, election and rejection. Men are the objects of election only in Him. From this flows disequilibrium and disproportion of the double predestination. Man as such does not deserve the divine Yes but only incurs on himself the wrath of the divine No. But he is the immediate object of election therefore divine Yes and No come to him in reverse order. He, of course, hears divine No, but never as ultimate word but always as penultimate one. Divine Yes comes to sinful man as his real and final predestination.

Karl Barth's Doubts about John Calvin's Assurance

> When we say that God elected as His own portion the negative side of the divine predestination, the reckoning with man's weakness and sin and inevitable punishment, we say implicitly that this portion is not man's portion. In so far, then, as predestination does contain a No, it is not a No spoken against man. In so far as it does involve exclusion and rejection, it is not the exclusion and rejection of man. In so far as it is directed to perdition and death, it is not directed to the perdition and death of man. All this things could come upon man and should come upon him, because by his unreliability as a creature, and more particularly by his demonstrated disloyalty as a sinful creature, he has clearly shown that he is quite unusable in the hands of God. He has clearly shown that he is not worthy of trust as a covenant-partner with God. From all eternity God could have excluded man from this covenant... But He did not do so (166).

And we know why 'He did not do so'. The Christian God is not the all-forgiving Deity of the Russian Orthodox theology who overlooks sin because of His infinite love and mercy. On the contrary, God treats sin seriously. He summons man to render an account, and He does not find an excuse for his sin. God is just, therefore he wills to treat sin seriously, to judge it and to sentence it, to reject and to condemn its author, delivering him over to death. Nevertheless God justifies sinners. And this justification is the irreversible Yes of election, the ultimate content of predestination.

> The justification of the sinner in Jesus Christ is the content of predestination in so far as predestination is a No and signifies rejection. On this side, too, it is eternal. It cannot be overthrown or reversed. Rejection cannot again become the portion or affair of man. The exchange which took place on Golgotha, when God chose as His throne the malefactor's cross, when the Son of God bore what the son of man ought to have borne, took place once and for all in fulfillment of God's eternal will, and it can never be reversed. There is no condemnation – literally none – for those that are in Christ Jesus. For this reason faith in the divine predestination as such and *per se* means faith in the non-rejection of man, or disbelief in his rejection. Man is not rejected. In God's eternal purpose it is God Himself who is rejected in His own Son...

Karl Barth

Predestination means that from all eternity God has determined upon man's acquittal at His own cost (167).

On this point Barth is not unclear. When he says that there is a disproportion between Yes and No of election he really means universal election of men and impossibility that any men are or will be rejected. 'We are no longer free to think of God's eternal election as bifurcating into a rightward and a leftward election. There is a leftward election. But God willed that the object of this election should be Himself and not man' (172). This thought is often repeated without any shadow of figurative speaking or exaggeration. And such statements can be understood only literally because they all result from the teaching about election of Jesus Christ to suffering. There is a very solid, serious and unshakable basis under each of Barth's assertions like 'the real foreordination of man is to attestation of the divine glory, to blessedness and to eternal life' (171). Men are not rejected because Jesus Christ has been rejected in their stead. Rejection of men can be thinkable only if one forgets about the rejection which Jesus Christ experienced. So long as the cross of Golgotha stands in the theology of Barth as the place where Son of God bore the punishment deserved by men we must take his statements about universal election at their face value. Otherwise we may despair to understand anything at all in Barth's theology.

The discussion of universal election inevitably raises the problem of universal salvation to which we will direct our attention after briefly outlining the fourth point of difference between traditional and 'purified' supralapsarianism.

Fourth, decretum absolutum. In the 'Supra-Infra' controversy 'all parties were agreed in their understanding of the divine Good pleasure which decided between election and rejection... They agreed, then, in thinking that this good-pleasure must be understood wholly and utterly as *decretum absolutum*. It is an act of divine freedom whose basis and meaning are completely hidden, and in their hiddenness must be regarded and reverenced as holy' (134).

As we have seen in the beginning of the chapter Barth does not reject the mystery of election. There is a mystery. But there is no *decretum absolutum*. Instead, there is Jesus Christ, electing God and elected man. Therefore the character of the mystery is radically changed. The mystery of *decretum absolutum* lies in the fact that both God and man are unknown quantities of an equation (146). We do not know the content of the divine decision. But it is not so if the absolute decree is replaced by the name of Jesus Christ. 'The will of God is Jesus Christ, and this will is known to us in the revelation of Jesus Christ' (157). The real mystery, according to Barth, lies in the fact that God made this eternal decision of election at all and not in the fact that we do not know anything about this decision except that it has been taken. 'Of all ideas, it is the one which is in itself unthinkable, the one which is thinkable only in faith and by the miraculous power of the Holy Spirit: that God himself should himself become the Son of Man in His eternal Son... If there is any mystery of God, if there is any secret which, even as we know it and it is revealed to us, still proclaims and characterizes itself more and more as a secret, then this is it' (159).

Thus the purified Supralapsarianism consists in belief that election is the primal decision of God which determines that there will be history between God and man and determines everything about this history. The object of election is one concrete man, Jesus Christ, which implies on the one hand that there is no fixed decision about the destiny of particular individuals and on the other hand that particular individuals are not rejected by God because rejection was directed to and exhausted itself in the person of Jesus Christ. Hence the only mystery of election which remains lies in the wonder of God's love, that God elected Jesus Christ and us in Him.

The Problem of Universalism

The question which concerns us in this section is whether Barth makes the step from universal election to universal salvation. It is strange that such a question arises at all since from the logical point of view there can be no dichotomy between the two. However the last part of *Church Dogmatics*, the fifth volume on eschatology, has never been written therefore we have to ask this question.

Karl Barth

The experts in the theology of Karl Barth give us the following answers. Gerrit Berkouwer, who wrote *The Triumph of Grace in the Theology of Karl Barth* in 1956, suggested that at that time Barth was at cross-roads:

> At this point Barth stands at a cross-roads in his thinking. He can move to the right or to the left, not in terms of the demands of a logical system, but in terms of centrally religious considerations. The one way that is open is that of the apokatastasis in which the reality of the divine decision which has been taken is without qualification declared to be identical with universality of reconciliation.
>
> The other way is that of *renewed* reflection on the seriousness of the human decision which, according to the overwhelming testimony of Scripture, is associated with the kerugma that goes out to the world.
>
> Up to now [1956], Barth has rejected the first possibility. To accept the apokatastasis would, in his view, make the existential seriousness of God's decision turn election into a self-evident matter and prejudice man's subjection to election as *grace*.
>
> Barth has not entered the second way either. He has indeed impressively shown the relationship of faith to salvation but, on the score of unbelief, his conception makes him oppose sharply the idea that it is a 'possibility'.
>
> So long as Barth declines to accept either alternative, however, he must remain standing at the crossroads. This standstill characterizes the present situation in his theology on the score of the universality of the triumph (290).

Another scholar of Karl Barth, Colin Brown, writing before death of Barth but after the book of Berkouwer, says in 1967:

> If this line of thought brings Barth to the brink of universalism, he hesitates to take the final step. On the one hand, he takes in an all-inclusive sense such biblical passages as Colossians 1:19f,; John 1:9, 29; 3:16f.; 4:42; 6:33; 8:12; 9:5; 11:9; 12:46; 2 Corinthians 5:19; 1 Timothy 2:4; and 1 John 2:2. But on the other hand, Barth shrinks from compromising the sovereign freedom of God by committing himself either to universal salvation of all mankind or to limited atonement for an elect number. Hence a certain air of ambiguity surrounds his

teaching. Although Barth's detailed study of the last things has yet to appear, it would seem that his way of resolving the difficulty lies along the line of the hint contained in the last sentence of the above extract ['Man takes upon him something which God has reserved for Himself if he tries to enter into this predestination or to think himself as predestined to sin and death']. Man as such can never be rejected. Man as such can never know the wrath and desolation which Christ knew on the cross. For Christ has taken it all upon Himself... This doctrine would appear to be the logical conclusion of the traditional Arminian interpretation of the atonement that on the cross Christ died for all men (132-133).

If Berkouwer could not say whether or not universal salvation would be Barth's position Brown thinks that Barth should inevitably come to this position. The more recent scholarly opinion states:

Does this amount to the doctrine of *apokatastasis* or universalism? In his written response to this question Barth refused to give a straight answer: 'I do not teach it, but I also do not not teach it!' Nevertheless, we guess what the answer must be. As Catholic scholar Hans Urs von Balthasar pointed out, 'it is clear from Barth's presentation of the doctrine of election that universal salvation is not only possible but inevitable. The only definitive reality is grace, and any condemnatory judgment has to be merely provisional' (Grenz, Olson 75).

In contradiction of the all above stated opinions we turn to the testimony of Barth himself. By the end of the chapter VII in *Church Dogmatics,* II/2, he says:

The election of each individual involves, and his calling completes, an opening up and enlargement of the (in itself) closed circle of the election of Jesus Christ and His community in relation to the world... The existence of each elect mans a hidden but real crossing of frontiers, to the gain of the kingdom of God as the kingdom of grace. It is the concern of God that there should be these frontier-crossing. It is also His concern how and when they should take place... It is His concern what is to be the final extent of the circle. If we are to respect the freedom of divine grace, we cannot venture the statement that it must and will finally be coincident with the world of man as such (as in the doctrine of the so-called *apokatastasis*). No such right or necessity can legitimately be deduced. Just as the gracious God does not need to elect or call any single man, so He does not need to elect or call all mankind... But, again, in grateful recognition of the grace of the divine freedom we cannot venture the opposite statement that there cannot and will not be this final opening up and enlargement of the circle of election and calling... We avoid both these statements, for they are both abstract and therefore cannot be any part of the message of Christ, but only formal conclusions without any actual substance (417-418).

In the lecture *The Humanity of God* delivered in 1956 Barth looks back across forty years of his theological work and appraises the reaction against 19th century liberal theology. By the end of the lecture he raises the question, 'Does this mean universalism?' and gives the following answer:

I wish here to make only three short observations, in which one is to detect no position for or against that which passes among us under this term.

1. One should not surrender himself in any case to the panic which this word seems to spread abroad, before informing himself exactly concerning its possible sense or non-sense.

2. One should at least be stimulated by the passage, Colossians 1:19, which admittedly states that God has determined through His Son as His image and as the first-born of the whole Creation to "reconcile all things (*ta panta*) to himself," to consider whether the concept could not perhaps have a good meaning. The same can be said of parallel passages.

3. ...This much is certain, that we have no theological right to set any sort of limits to the loving-kindness of God which has appeared in Jesus Christ. Our theological duty is to see and understand it as being still greater than we had seen before (61-62).

The suggestion of the present author is that the tension which we encounter in Barth's doctrine of election is consistent with the doctrine itself and is deliberate. To imitate Barth's manner of speaking, this is a case of a consistent inconsistency. We suggest that Berkouwer was not exactly right when he expected Barth to leave the crossroads behind and called his position 'standstill'. We also suggest that Brown and Grenz and Olson said more than they could when they recognized the tension and then asserted that this tension must be solved in direction of universalism. As the last two quotes from Barth himself indicate he had no intention to move beyond the crossroad either to apokatastasis or final rejection of some men. It is in line with one of his corrections of Supralapsarianism: the eternal destinies of individual men are not fixed by any pre-temporal decree. Therefore we may venture to state that one of the innovations of Barth's doctrine of election consists precisely in this: overcoming the direct relation between eternal decree of God and personal salvation. Barth's theology eliminates this issue as having no meaning. The destiny of each man is decided in time on the basis of election of Jesus Christ before, in and after time.

In conclusion, with regards to the discussion of the problem of universalism in Barth's theology we suggest that it is arguable that this problem originates in or is at least analogous to the Calvinistic doctrine of limited atonement. In order to see it we need only to remind ourselves that universal election of Barth is based on substitutionary rejection of Jesus Christ. No man is rejected only because Jesus Christ bore the punishment of rejection in His own person on the cross of Golgotha. His rejection was real and not imaginary, the wrath, the judgment, the punishment of God has been really poured on Him. Therefore how can God reject any particular man?

Is this not exactly the problem of atonement in orthodox theology? Brown thinks that Barth solves the dilemma of atonement in the Arminian direction, but is this judgment fair? Can we really charge Barth who insisted so strongly on the freedom of grace in election with Arminian synergism? We doubt it. We rather suggest that Barth in his own way came to the well-known Calvinistic statement: 'Sufficient for all, efficient for elect'. As traditional Calvinistic theology cannot answer the question for whom Christ died so Barth refuses to answer the question whether the whole world will be saved. As a Calvinist pastor assures his hearers after they believed in the gospel that they may be certain that Christ died for them so Barth is able to assure believers that their election consist in faith in Jesus Christ: '...their election consists concretely in their faith in Him' (126). It is exactly the problem of extent of the atonement which we meet in Barth's denial of universalism. As Calvinist theologians cannot answer the question how is it possible that the death of Christ is only sufficient for all without being efficient for all so Barth cannot answer the question how 'universally meaning and efficacious' (117) election of Christ leaves the question of universalism open. The evasive Calvinistic formulation 'sufficient for all, efficient for elect' may as well be charged with Arminian synergism as Barth's refusal to make step from universal election to universal salvation.

The analogy of limited atonement and Barth's doctrine of election may not be fully valid. We do not have space to develop the comparison. However one thing is clear: the deliberate inconsistency of Barth's doctrine of election is not without parallel in the history of theology, even orthodox theology. The problem it creates for preaching Christ is comparable to the problem created by the doctrine of limited atonement.

The Doctrine of Assurance

In this section we want outline Barth's doctrine of assurance as the corollary of his doctrine of election. We will begin with his critique of the traditional doctrine of assurance and then will outline his own positive teaching.

First, critique of the Reformed doctrine of assurance. Barth elucidates Calvin's doctrine of assurance comparing it with the doctrine of inner testimony of the Holy Spirit about the truthfulness of Bible (334). As is well-known Calvin believed in self-authentication of the Holy Scripture. Our faith in the Bible as the very word of God does not depend on rational proofs but is born out of direct testimony of the Holy Spirit. As we read or hear the content of the Bible we, under the influence of the Holy Spirit, come to sure conviction that we read or hear the word of God. The rational proofs of the divine origin of Scriptures have only secondary importance: on one hand, faith is not based on reason, on the other reason does not contradict our faith

Karl Barth's Doubts about John Calvin's Assurance

but rather confirms it after we came to belief in divinity of the Bible. The same applies in Calvin, says Barth, to assurance of personal salvation. Faith and assurance are born under the influence of the Holy Spirit out of direct promise of Christ. The testimony of our works have only secondary importance: assurance is not based on self-examination but the evidence of grace in life may support assurance. However Barth detects a problem in Calvin which according to Barth, Calvin did not perceive himself (339):

> As Christ is certainly the source and object of faith, so Christ Himself is assuredly lives and works in the believer through faith, and is one with him. But this being the case, it is inevitable that we should understand faith itself and the believer as such and his human life an incidental, but certainly not on that account superfluous, confirmation of the one, decisive witness. A man is sure that this is established in itself, and is true, by its own weight, and therefore in the power of the witness of Jesus Christ and the Holy Spirit. But he is so only in the form of his own decision, his own faith and confession, his own corresponding being. Christ cannot be to him a witness of his election without his receiving His witness, and therefore himself becoming a bearer of this witness (334).

In other words, in Calvin's thought, man himself is the final witness of his election and the basis of his assurance.

> The final witness of Jesus Christ to each individual, the least independent and least worthy of hearing, yet the most indispensable in this situation and function, is the individual himself. While his witness in and by itself does not give him the slightest assurance, he cannot receive the witness of Jesus Christ and the Holy Spirit – which gives real and complete assurance – unless he receives to from himself, unless he himself gives it in his faith and life and works. It is as I live as an elect man that I am and shall be assured of my election (335).

The critique of Barth is similar to that of Cunningham but of course it does not take the simplistic form of syllogistic argument. Unlike Cunningham, Barth believes that Calvin's doctrine of assurance has certain undeniable advantages.

Karl Barth

The merit of Calvin in formulating his problematic doctrine of assurance is threefold (335-336). First, he taught that the testimony of 'works' must not take the first place and assume the role of a crown witness. Second, the testimony of 'works' in Calvin was never separated from faith. According to Calvin, says Barth, 'It is not to be treated as a self-supporting decision of empirical self-examination and self-evaluation, distinguishable from the testimony of faith (and from Jesus Christ Himself) or from the testimony of the Holy Spirit' (336). Third, Calvin did not detach the testimony of 'works' from the self-testimony of Christ, from the promise of forgiveness of sins, or in general from the objective Word of God, as if it had the power in itself to penetrate its mystery.

The heirs of Calvin made a fatal mistake of destroying the unstable balance in Calvin's theology between the self-testimony of Christ and the testimony of works. According to Barth, such men as Beza did understand the problem created by Calvin's doctrine of assurance, but they wanted 'to think the matter systematically through to a conclusion'. As the result they abandoned Calvin's caution about the testimony of works and formulated the practical syllogism moving the self-testimony of the life of the elect to the first place and giving it an independent place alongside the testimony of Jesus Christ (336).

At this point Barth asks a very important question, 'whether by taking this course they merely fell victim to an accidental error, or whether this was a necessary aberration within the framework of the basic view common both to Calvin and themselves' (336). The foreseeable answer is that Calvin did not fell himself into this error only because the dilemma between self-testimony of Christ and necessity of final testimony of man's life 'escaped him', and that the step taken by Beza and others was 'actually unavoidable in the context of the common basic view which they all [Calvin and his theological heirs] shared' (338). After this comes an important conclusion: 'The need for a total revision of the dogma [of election] is plainly shown by the history of this subsidiary problem' (339). By the 'total revision' we obviously ought to understand the innovation of Barth which consists in the change of the object of election.

Second, Barth's doctrine of assurance. As we just have seen Barth thinks that Calvin's doctrine of assurance is paradoxically correct: Calvin correctly maintained that assurance may be based only on the self-testimony of Christ which we accept in faith but did not understand that in his own doctrine of election contradicted his doctrine of assurance. In other words, Calvin fortunately did not realize that it is impossible to believe in *decretum absolutum* which eternally fixed destiny of a particular man and at the same time teach that assurance is based on the promise of Christ and not on practical syllogism. Beza saw the problem and solved it in direction of *syllogismus practicus*. Barth not only saw the contradiction in Calvin's teaching but unlike Beza he knew how overcome it without falling into latter's error. Barth argues that in order to maintain Calvin doctrine of assurance and remove the contradiction involved one has to interpret election Christologically and replace the absolute decree with Jesus Christ.

> Our conclusion is, then, that Calvin's problem of the self-assurance of the elect can and actually must be tackled, but that the caution with which Calvin dealt with it can and actually must be maintained. In the setting of the classical doctrine the one could take place only at the expense of the other. But in a setting of the doctrine of predestination which has a Christological basis there is room for both and both are needed (340).

Since the basis of election is Jesus Christ, the elect who came to believe in Christ is himself the witness of his own election (339). This means three things. First, 'the fact that the elect is himself a witness to his election means that he himself may witness to the election of Jesus Christ, and to his own election in and with it... although he participates in this witness as a bearer as well as a recipient, he does so simply as *adminiculum inferius* of the testimony itself, and even as only by its own inner power, in the inexpressible power of the grace of Jesus Christ' (339). In other words the witness of faith is secondary but indispensable. Second, 'his participation in this witness and therefore his assurance about himself, can have absolutely nothing to do with self-examination and self-evaluation' (339). Third, 'as the elect man is in this way assured of his election, he is indeed aware of a mysterious correspondence (even identity), not between the hidden counsel of God and the condition of his own piety and morality, but between the election of Jesus Christ and the miracle of the actual fulfillment of his faith' (340).

Barth's doctrine boils down to this. The basis of assurance is that Jesus Christ is the electing God and the elected man. When one comes to believe in Him he understands that he has been elected in Jesus Christ. His faith witnesses to him about his election in Jesus Christ but faith itself is not the primary but only secondary basis of assurance of being elect. The immediate basis of assurance is the election of Jesus Christ. Works cannot be the basis of assurance too. The life of the elect with its faith and works may only inspire wonder because of the miracle of his election.

We should also add that Barth endorses the traditional doctrine of perseverance of the saints. He believes in constancy of faith of the elect and does not believe that it can be finally lost. Eternal life is the unquestionable perspective of the elect.

> Since God cannot deceive Himself, cannot be conjured, and cannot be unfaithful either to Himself or to us, it is of the essence of election that there can be no fundamental eternal reversal. The Yes of God to His elect cannot be transformed into an absolute No. Because, then they have the absolute divine Yes in their ears and in their hearts, they both may and should be assured in faith of their election, and therefore of eternal salvation – not in harmony with their evil human No to God, but in spite of it, and in this way in genuine and successful conflict with it... If the faith of the elect lives with Jesus Christ as its basis and with Jesus Christ as its goal, it is impossible to see how it can be absolutely lost... Can we more effectively cheapen faith than by denying its constancy? (332).

As strange as our conclusion may sound we have to state that universal salvation is emphatically not the basis of personal assurance in Barth's theology. It is so for the simple reason that Barth did not teach universalism. Quite unexpectedly the basis of assurance is the divine promise of grace which is contained in the election of

Jesus Christ and which we appropriate by faith. Faith informs us that we are elected in Jesus Christ and on the basis of this information we are sure of acceptance with God. Believing in the election of Jesus Christ we may be sure that we are elected for fellowship with God. Believing in the election of Jesus Christ we be sure of eternal life because the rejection which is ours has been forever removed by Jesus Christ in His own person and has nothing to do with us anymore. Jesus Christ in whom we are elected for glory and in whom our rejection is rejected is the basis of assurance of the present forgiveness of sins and of the future eternal life.

A Broader Theological Context

Berkouwer gives a brilliant analysis of Barth's theology in his book *The Triumph of Grace in the Theology of Karl Barth*. This book was even acknowledged by Barth himself as the best book on himself (Brown 154). We will use Berkouwer's work as the main secondary source and follow its order of discussion of Barth's theology adding to it insights from other books on Barth. This overview will protect us from misunderstanding Barth's doctrine of election and assurance.

Berkouwer suggests looking at Barth's theology in terms of the 'triumph of grace', an idea he thinks (according to Barth himself, wrongly) unites different aspect of Barth's thought. He evaluates Barth's doctrine of grace from four points of view. First, it should be asked, 'Over which darkness does the light of God's grace triumph?' (213) In other words, the question is, What is sin? Second, 'What is the place of faith in this triumph?' Third, What does the 'divine character of the triumph' mean? The doctrine of reconciliation is to be considered under this heading. Finally, we should pay attention to Barth's 'conception of eternal life'. 'Although the discussion of these four aspects of Barth's theology does not by any means present a complete analysis and evaluation of it, we believe that it does confront us with the central questions of his dogmatics...' (213-214).

Karl Barth

Sin and grace

From Barth's point of view sin is impossible. The question is in what of two senses we should understand this impossibility: noetic or ontic? The noetic impossibility of sin means that we cannot comprehend the origin and existence of sin. The ontic impossibility means that sin cannot exist as a reality of human life. Traditional approach to the enigma of sin assumed on the biblical grounds that the first man Adam was a historical person who had free will, and that he could choose between obeying and disobeying God's will. He disobeyed, he fell and in this way evil and sin entered the world of human beings. God was not taken unaware by the Fall. He knew it was going to happen, he permitted it to happen, he ordained it to happen but he is not the author of sin. Traditional enigma of sin is noetic: we do not understand how the Fall could happen, why Adam made the fatal choice, and how God is not the author of sin.

However Barth speaks about ontological impossibility of sin. He rejects the idea of free will. God did not give man ability to choose between obeying ad disobeying him. He was given freedom which consisted in ability to choose God's will. The possibility of going against God's will was denied to man. Therefore the Fall could not happen, sin is an impossible possibility.

> Barth... emphatically opposes the idea that in creating man God created also the 'possibility' of his fall. He rejects the idea that man was created with the 'possibility' of sinning, of choosing between good and evil, the possibility of liberum arbitrum... the freedom that is given to man is not 'freedom of choice between obedience and disobedience'. Precisely that freedom is denied him... When God gives man freedom He gives him freedom exclusively for the purpose of being truly obedient... It cannot be said that sin could, 'according to God's will, take place.' But man was vulnerable and things have come to the actuality of threat from the side of chaos. Sin has become reality, horrible reality. But the choice which man made was irrational, absurd, it was the impossible possibility of sin. Sin can only be describe as absurd, irrational. A real ground for it there is not. It has no possibility other than the possibility of the impossible (61-62).

Karl Barth's Doubts about John Calvin's Assurance

It means that Barth redefines the traditional understanding of the mystery of sin.

> Here it becomes plain why, for Barth, sin is a mystery. This mystery, this enigma, has nothing to do with the limits of our understanding, in the sense of the noetic incomprehensibility of sin. The mystery consists in the fact that sin is something which in the very nature of the case cannot be. This is the heart of Barth's doctrine of sin, which can be summarized in that strange expression: the ontological impossibility of sin (225-226).
>
> The difference between Barth and the general conception of the Church and of theology on the score of the origin of sin lies in this, that for Barth sin not only has a mysterious, incomprehensible character, but is an ontological impossibility. This is not a problem of our knowledge of sin, but of sin itself. It is a violation f grace, but of that grace which because of God's election in Jesus is inviolable (228).

Berkouwer suggests that Barth's terminology should be rejected because it contradicts biblical language.

> His conception of 'impossibility' is unacceptable because the Bible speaks in a wholly different way about the 'reality' of sin. When sin and godlessness are designated in terms of a divine accusation of utter seriousness and sin is related to man's responsibility and to death, any and every use of the concept 'impossibility' and particularly 'ontological impossibility' as a speculative effort to speak where Scripture does not speak is unwarranted. We do not suggest, therefore, that by 'impossibility' Barth means 'unreality'; we wish rather to reject the word in the sense in which Barth uses it... Barth excludes the ability to sin from the good nature with which man was created. Having done this, however, he again asserts this "ability" (as an insane ability) because of the reality of sin in the world. This creates a peculiar tension which we find nowhere in the Bible (233).

Sin is impossible not only because the ability to sin is excluded from the good nature with which man was created but also because sin has already been conquered by God's grace in election and reconciliation. Van Til says:

Karl Barth

We see that the freedom and universality of grace are involved in Christ as the elected man. For as such he is, from eternity, the one who has borne the wrath of God for all men. Thus we have the objective completion of the work of redemption for all men once for all, because from eternity it was accomplished in Christ. Sin becomes impossible possibility for other men. Man is to be defined as that being who is the object of God's grace. The real man is the one who participates with Christ as the victor over Chaos (41).

Thus, though impossible and insane, the possibility of sin was actualized in men. Sin had already been neutralized and conquered by the election of Jesus Christ. Moreover, the ontological impossibility of sin should be understood Christologically. In other words, the inherent inability of man to sin should be explained in terms of grace revealed in Christ. Berkouwer says: 'We see that the triumph of grace is emphatically placed before sin and that for this reason sin is anticipated and intercepted and so made ontologically impossible. The triumph of grace is the reverse side of (in a certain sense one can say that it is identical with) the ontological impossibility of sin' (234). Chaos and sin are powerless and only apparently dangerous. They exist, but they do not really exist because God denied them existence in creation as well as by means of reconciliation. Their existence is the matter of the past. The ultimate threat of chaos and sin – alienation from God – cannot be realized because of the divine No to the kingdom of darkness. Berkouwer concludes that in Barth's theology we find an ultimate and irreversible triumph of grace over sin:

> The chaos has therefore been rejected in Jesus Christ and through this rejection it has been 'emptied.' One can now think of the chaos only in an a-posteriori fashion, one can think of it only by way of 'glancing back' to it. The only role which the chaos can still play is the role of a defeated enemy.
>
> How it is possible that it is all past – in Christ – and that at the same time the chaos can still play a role n the affairs of men? This is possibility only because we must assume that the power of the chaos of which we are still aware is not true power. We can ascribe to it 'only the force of dangerous appearance.' In reality, i.e., in Jesus Christ, the power of the chaos has been

broken, emptied, judged. This holds true for the significance of the chaos for the entire cosmos, and even though we do not see this, it is nevertheless true, for the victory has taken place and is in need neither of improvement nor of repetition. The kingdom of chaos is a shadow-kingdom which has been 'objectively put away.' That it still 'does' anything is the world is only 'because of the blindness of our eyes.' God permits that we can not yet see His kingdom and that we 'to that extent still find ourselves pressed by the chaos.' He permits the chaos to be an 'apparently effective force.' But it is not a dangerous force. 'In this no longer dangerous form of a reminiscence and shadow of its former power it is an instrument of God's willing and doing.' God considers it good that we live 'as though' the kingdom of chaos has not yet come to an end. But, actually, through the triumph of grace the chaos is not more' (75).

From the point of view of Berkouwer in light of Barth's doctrine of sin it becomes clear that universalism is not only a logical conclusion from Barth's peculiar doctrine of election. The charge with apokatastasis may be rejected only at the expense of weakening the doctrine of the triumph of grace over sin and at expense of emptying of any sense the statements about 'apparent' reality, power and threat of chaos. From Barth's point of view 'sin is the futile effort of man to resists the grace of God in Christ. Its defeat is therefore certain in advance' (Van Til 104). However, the sinful effort of man is not futile, the power and the threat of chaos are not apparent but very real if the ultimate salvation of all men is not guaranteed. If one seriously holds to the idea that sin is an impossible possibility which even if actualized in an insane and satanic way has been already conquered by grace in Christ, then it is quite irrational to deny that sin can ultimately alienate any man from his Creator and Redeemer God.

This sounds very true and logical, and the conclusion drawn by Berkouwer seems to be inevitable. The only thing of which we should constantly remind ourselves is that Barth deliberately and consistently refused to say the final word on the apokatastasis issue. Therefore we cannot make for Barth the step from ultimate triumph of grace over sin to universal salvation.

Karl Barth

Faith

Barth's understanding of faith is strikingly similar to Calvin's. The question is whether this similarity is formal or essential? One of Barth's American lectures published in the book *Evangelical Theology: An Introduction* is titled 'Faith' (the quotes from Barth in this section are from this book). Hopefully Barth presents an adequate report of his own doctrine. But it must be admitted that in the lecture he considers faith from a particular point of view: what is faith which is required for theological undertaking.

Faith is an event. 'What happens in the event of faith is that the Word of God frees one man among many for faith itself... By God's Word, together with the life giving power and the unique sovereignty of the Spirit, one man among many is permitted to exists continually as a free man' (100). A man who has faith is the man who is free to affirm, to put trust in and be obedient to the Word of God (101). As an event, faith is not something man gains once for all. This event is to be repeated continually, every morning: 'For this very reason he [believer] will not suppose that he has his faith but he will hope and hope and hope for it as the Israelites hoped afresh every morning for the manna in the wilderness. And when he receives this faith afresh, he will also daily activate it anew' (105).

Faith has a noetic dimension: '...faith has the fundamental character of knowledge' (101). But faith is emphatically not human knowledge and exactly because of this faith is the most certain knowledge.

> [F]aith would not doubt be a somewhat petty event, scarcely worth mentioning in this context, if what was meant by it was a human notion... Faith in this object [God], therefore, is not hypothetical and problematic knowledge. It is quite basically a most intensive, strict, and certain knowledge. Compared with it, even what is supposedly the most certain knowledge on our side of the human boundary can only be esteemed a hypothesis – perhaps useful, but fundamentally beset by problems (97-98).

Faith is more than a mere intellectual belief although the believer has certain convictions which come out of his faith.

Karl Barth's Doubts about John Calvin's Assurance

Faith is a history, new every morning. It is no state or attribute. It should not be confuse with the mere capacity and willingness to believe. Of course, it may result in and involve all sorts of faithfully held convictions [like virgin birth, descent into hell, resurrection of the flesh]... All the same, willingness to believe all those and similar points is not yet faith. Faith is no *credere quod*, but rather a *credere in*, according to the unmistakable formulation of the Apostle's Creed; it is not a belief 'that...' but a faith 'in...' – in God himself, the God of the Gospel who is Father, Son, and Spirit... Yet faith is not a matter of being full of "belief" in and on such special issues. Instead, what is important is believing in him, God himself... (103-104).

Faith is related to promise: 'First of all, faith is definitely no such venture as that which Satan, for instance, suggested to the Lord on the pinnacle of the temple (Luke 4:9-12). It is, instead, a sober as well as a brave appropriation of a firm and certain promise' (102).

Faith is possible only because of the illumination by Holy Spirit: Whoever believes, knows and confesses that he cannot 'by his own understanding and power' in any way believe. He will simply perform this believing, without losing sight of the unbelief that continually accompanies him and makes itself felt. Called and illumined by the Holy Spirit as he is, he does not understand himself; he cannot help but completely wonder at himself. He will say 'I believe' only in and with the entreaty, 'Lord, help my unbelief' (104-105).

Finally, faith is assailed by doubts. 'The criterion of the genuineness and enduring capacity of the faith which is indispensable to the theologian is not its special strength, depth, or fervor. It does not matter that this faith will, as a rule, be rather weak and delicate, fluttering in the windy currents of life and its accidents' (104).

Except for the idea that faith is an event, Barth's understanding of faith resembles that of Calvin. Both Calvin and Barth understood faith as knowledge which is more sure than any sort of knowledge obtained by reason. The content of this knowledge is the revelation of grace and promise in Jesus Christ. Illumination of the Holy Spirit is absolutely necessary for obtaining faith. Finally, doubts are not excluded from the experience of the true believer.

However, the analysis of Barth by Berkouwer gives an impression that in Barth's understanding of faith the noetic dimension is dominant. Faith is acceptance of certain facts; acknowledgement of truth about God revealed in Jesus Christ. Berkouwer says:

> Man must seek refuge at Golgotha because Christ has borne the judgment. That is the stimulus to all missionary labor. 'The heart of the confession of the New Testament is the consummated judgment of God in the death of Jesus Christ on the cross. No other man stands in this center, none other stands so truly in God's judgment.' All other men stand 'around this center'. There is one remarkable difference among them, however: 'the Christian knows, the others do not yet know.' The apostles knew that the judgment had been executed, others did not yet know the true state of affairs... The contrast between the knowing in the Church and the not-knowing in the world is the motive, and the bridging of the chasm between the two is the problem, of the witness of the early Church (120).

Berkouwer goes as far as comparing preaching with delivering information and the act of believing with acquiring information:

> The 'not yet knowing' plays a decisive role in Barth's thinking... In this conception, which continually recurs in the writings of Barth, the proclamation can hardly be otherwise understood as a giving of 'information' about a given state of affairs, about a already taken decision which is 'made known' in the proclamation. We do not wish to deny that Barth gives a place to the hortatory aspect of the proclamation by means of another emphasis, namely, through the 'open situation' of the proclamation. But this does not alter the fact that his conception of the already taken decision leaves room for the proclamation only in the sense of an informative declaration concerning the accomplished fact of God's decisive grace for all (265, 275-6).

Karl Barth's Doubts about John Calvin's Assurance

Reconciliation

Berkouwer starts discussion of Barth's doctrine of reconciliation with a statement about revelation of God in Christ. 'Through the man Jesus Christ, God Himself is revealed as the divine subject in the work of Christ. This conception brings us to the heart of Barth's doctrine of reconciliation' (123). This statement gives an impression that God's revelation in Christ is very closely related to the reconciliation which he accomplished through Christ. In the light of the subsequent treatment of the doctrine of reconciliation a suspicion arises that for Barth reconciliation is not only related to revelation in Christ but that revelation and reconciliation are identical.

Discussing Barth's doctrine of reconciliation Berkouwer covers a number of important themes in his theology. If we reject natural theology and accept only that knowledge about God which comes to us in Christ then 'it becomes possible to see the "God Himself" in the reconciling work of God in Christ' (126). For example, 'It no longer belongs to the impossibilities of thought to see "God Himself" in Christ in the most ultimate humiliation, powerlessness and self-surrender...' (126). Then, also, the act of obedience of Christ is obedience of God himself (130). Still another conclusion may be drawn from the fact that in Christ we find God Himself, namely, that 'humiliation and exaltation cannot be temporally separated from each other but must be seen together in the one deed of reconciliation' (133).

The mentioned aspects of Barth's doctrine of reconciliation are important, they may throw new light on incarnation, nonetheless in Berkouwer's treatment of Barth's doctrine of reconciliation the most important element is missing. Orthodox theology since Anselm understood reconciliation in terms of the sacrificial death of Christ on the cross. Berkouwer mentions Barth's position on this only in passing in a footnote in section in which he discusses resurrection of Christ!

> This *grace*-character of Christ's resurrection is essential to Barth's Christology. It is clear that this thought is most closely related to other views of Barth about the punitive sufferings of Christ... Concerning the concept 'punishment' Barth writes, with reference to Isaiah 53, 'It is therefore not to be wholly rejected. But it may not become a major concept as it did for Anselm and certainly not

in the sense of satisfaction with respect to the wrath of God. This last idea is wholly foreign to the New Testament' (138).

The suspicion which the opening phrases of the chapter on reconciliation raised proved to be not without ground. Barth understands reconciliation in terms of incarnation which is the means of God's self-revelation. Van Til says that for Barth 'Jesus Christ is reconciliation... The existence of Jesus Christ as truly God and truly man constitutes the finished act of man's reconciliation with God... the incarnation is reconciliation... Thus God can and does reveal himself in Jesus Christ. And therewith God has reconciled the world to himself' (16, 17, 19, 20).

Van Til is often a partial critic of Barth but in this analysis he appears to be right. Thomas F. Torrance, who is a follower of Barth, gives his own understanding of Barth's position on reconciliation:

Thus the oneness in being and agency between Christ and God must be understood from *soteriological* perspective...

The incarnation includes the whole life and activity of Jesus Christ culminating in his resurrection and ascension, while the atonement begins from his very conception and birth when he put on the form of a servant and began to pay the price of our redemption. As one Mediator between God and man, the man Christ Jesus is not only God with us, but God for us, God who has crossed chasm of alienation between us and himself, God who has taken our rebellious and corrupt human nature upon himself, God who has made our sin and quilt, our misery and death, our condemnation and godlessness, his very own, in order to intercede for us, to substitute himself in our place, bearing the just punishment of our sin, and offering and making restitution by suffering what we could not suffer and where we could make no restitution at all.

That is the doctrine of Jesus Christ as Mediator who is God of God and man of man in one Person, and who as such reconciles God to man and man to God in the hypostatic union of his divine and human natures. This hypostatic union, however, was the atoning union in Christ between the Holy One of God and our sinful humanity which he made his own but which, while making it his own, he healed and sanctified in his own sinless life (227, 229-230).

Karl Barth's Doubts about John Calvin's Assurance

If Torrance is correct then the orthodox doctrine of atonement in the blood of Christ (in spite of the fact that the traditional terminology is retained) is effectually jettisoned from Barth's thought. Thus for Barth redemption and reconciliation lie in the fact that God became man. It is not imputation of our sin to Christ on the cross and bearing of God's judgment by him but 'the hypostatic union of his divine and human natures' which really effects atonement. That Barth has not only added a new dimension to the doctrine of atonement extending it to the whole incarnate existence of the Son of God but also rejected the orthodox doctrine of propitiation is evident from the following passage in Torrance:

> Karl Barth's objection to most Western doctrines of the atonement was that they had resiled from this soteriological emphasis on the inner connection between incarnation and atonement... and kept interpreting the sacrifice of Christ on the cross mainly as the external transference of penalty between sinners and God, rather than as the culmination of God's incarnational penetration into the alienated roots of humanity in order to bear upon himself our judgment... (213).

Eternal life

Barth's doctrine of eternal life is one of the most shocking innovations of his theology. Berkouwer says that it is unique in the history of theology. 'Barth's conception of the "eternalizing" of our ending life has, so far as I know, no antecedents in the history of Christian doctrine' (158). The doctrine of 'eternalizing' is so unusual for Christian thought that Berkouwer thinks it is necessary to give a warning to his readers lest they terribly misunderstand Barth: 'What is certainly not meant [by the word 'eternalizing'] is the atheistic idea of "dead is dead"' (328). This is an interesting way to understand (or misunderstand) a Christian theologian!

The starting point of Barth's thought is the fact that man did not always exist. From this he concludes that he will not always exist. In other words, as there is the 'beginning time' in human life so there should the 'ending time'. 'There was a time in which we were not yet, as also there shall be time in which we shall not be any more. Human life lies between the poles of this two-fold not-being, the "being-not-yet" and the "being-no-longer"' (153).

Death belongs to human nature. As such, it is part of God's original good creation. 'The end of human life is not as such a symptom of "disorder" but of order, not a "chaotic reign of terror", but a good creation of God... According to God's good creation human life has a boundary' (161). Barth is quite unambiguous about the meaning of this 'boundary':

> We must... notice that Barth sharply opposes the idea of an extension of human life after death... There is no continuation, no further happening, after the sounding of the last trump... The hope that we have does not involve an extension of our life; its point of reference is our life as it has been. The life that has been, life in the limitations we have known, is 'eternalized', and this action upon the life that has been takes place in such a manner that it does not include a continuation of our finite existence in the future... This is the resurrection of the dead' (158).

In order to distinguish Barth doctrine of 'eternalizing' from the atheistic disbelief in life after death Berkouwer underscores that Barth himself insisted that man does not turn to nothing after death:

> He points out that the limitation of our earlier not-being stands in different category than our future being-no-longer. Death, empirical death, as we know it and as we know it will one day enter our own life, is not simply a neutral ending of our temporal existence. It is not a normal and 'natural' return to the not-being whence we came. It is return to God. We are not on the way to nothing or to neutral and empty being-no-more (155).

> Therefore man does not as such have a 'beyond,' nor does he need one, 'for God is his beyond.' There is no extension of his earthly temporalness. This thesis, Barth emphasizes, may under no circumstances be understood to mean that death means *finis* [dead is dead] and that there is no reason or room in life for hope and expectation. Also in his quality as having-been man is not nothing

but 'participates in the eternal life of God.' It is precisely his life on this side of death, his ending and dying life, that is glorified (160).

When Berkouwer comes to evaluation of Barth's doctrine of 'eternalizing' he rejects it as completely erroneous for two reasons. First, this doctrine is not based on Christology as Barth claims but rather on his anthropological presuppositions. 'Christological' argumentation of Barth runs as follows:

> Because Christ's death was the voluntary end of His human life, because it was the strange burden which did not originally belong to his life, His death was not anthropologically necessary. This fact reveals in Him, the true man, a being-human which is not necessarily to be identified with subjection to death as judgment. For this reason – this is the decisive turn in the argument – the fact of human death as such is not, as it was in the case of Christ, a judgment. The being-limited of man's life can therefore be regarded as belonging to man's good creation (336).

To this Berkouwer replies:

> It is difficult to escape the thought that this abstract discussion about the end of Jesus' life hardly constitutes a conclusion drawn from relationship of Christology to anthropology. It is not so much Christology as anthropology that is primary here. It is anthropology that primarily gives meaning to man's life as having a 'limited' time... In fact, in terms of Barth's own view one might rather conclude to a non-limited time of man's life since Christ is not only crucified one but also the risen and living Lord, the man Jesus Christ, who could explain, 'I died, and behold I am alive for evermore' (Rev 1:18). For this reason alone Barth's thesis drawn from the mortality of Jesus is untenable (336).

Second, this doctrine is not based on the witness of Scripture and even contradicts its 'very clear' teaching.

> In the light of our earthly time it is possible to speak, as also the Bible speaks, of a 'being-no-longer' with respect to this earthly life. It is not possible, however, to construe a definitive parallel in terms of this idea between our (earlier) 'not-being-yet' and our (later) 'no-longer-being.'

This parallel, in the definitive sense in which Barth posits it, is precisely the thing that Scripture denies us. It is not the idea of continuity that Scripture opposes, but the denial of it. This becomes very clear when Jesus speaks against the Sadducees who repudiated the doctrine of the resurrection of the dead (Matt. 22:23)...

Not only is the wrong idea of continuity rejected by Christ, however, but He also indicates their error and their not knowing the Scriptures and the power of God by pointing to Exodus 3:6 where God says at a time in which Abraham, Isaac, and Jacob are long since dead, 'I am the God of Abraham, and the God of Isaac, and the God of Jacob. He is not the God of the dead, but of the living' (Matt. 22:23).

The point of this answer lies in the continuity of their human life and from this it appears that it is precisely this continuity that includes the resurrection of the dead which had been called into question. There is no question of dropping away of 'my' in 'God is my beyond'. Rather eternal maintaining of it is emphasized (338-339).

Conclusion

As the secondary sources indicate Barth's doctrine of assurance is really a problematic one. Apart from the fact that Barth refuses to teach universalism as the logical conclusion of his doctrine of election and in this way endangers the basis of personal assurance in his thought, apart from the innovation by which Barth detaches divine election from the destiny of particular men denying the fixity of the eternal decree and in this way nurturing the suspicion that God may be a capricious tyrant, apart from these two difficulties Barth's doctrines of reconciliation and eternal life present two serious additional problems. First, if incarnation is reconciliation then the basis of non-rejection of men becomes dubious. It is no longer substitutionary sufferings and death of Christ on the cross of Golgotha that give us assurance that we are not rejected by God but unbiblical notion of 'God's incarnational penetration into the alienated roots of humanity' which assures us that the ontological gap between God and man is overcome.

Second, if eternal life is 'eternalizing' of the present life in sense of discontinuity of human existence and being present only in the mind of God then what kind of hope does the assurance of salvation gives us? Is there any sense in speaking about election to eternal life? What is the point of insisting that faith is characterized by constancy which guarantees salvation in the future? If analysis of Berkouwer is correct then everything Barth says about being elect, fellowship with God, forgiveness of sins belongs really only to this life. There is no life hereafter in any imaginable sense which can give us hope of and longing for it.

Perhaps exactly at this point the tension between universal election and universal salvation is to be solved. All men are elect in this earthly life. Barth asserts this without any reservation. Even unbelievers are not rejected – in this life. What will happen to unbelievers after death? This question is pointless – there is no life after death. Therefore Barth could say that he did not teach universalism and did not not teach it. He did teach universalism in that sense that all men are elect in this life. But he did not teach universalism in that sense that in the life hereafter some will enjoy fellowship with God while others will be in outer darkness. He could not possibly teach this kind of universal salvation because there is neither heaven nor hell after death.

Thus, if we may rely on the secondary sources, personal assurance of salvation in Barth's theology is devoid from the traditional orthodox point of view of any significance both in respect of its basis and its hope. It is neither possible to understand in what sense Jesus Christ took our rejection on Himself nor to imagine eternal existence of this present earthly life (if we are allowed to put it in this way) in the museum of the mind of God. Thus, Barth aiming to go beyond Calvin's doctrine of assurance reached the point of no-assurance. His doctrine of assurance is so ambiguous that it is unusable in pastoral ministry.

Karl Barth

And we want to underscore the ambiguous character of Barth's teaching. Perhaps, we misunderstood him: he did not deny propitiatory character of Christ's death and eternal life in the resurrected body. Nevertheless, he certainly made himself hard to understand and this limits application of his colossal theological work in congregational teaching. What his theology does very well is to provoke thought in those who want to think and to shake out of theological numbness those who is ready to reevaluate the traditional teaching. But a pastor after being provoked to thinking by Barth has the task of developing clear and unambiguous theological formulations for his own teaching ministry.

3. A Comparative Analysis of Calvin's and Barth's Doctrine of Assurance

In this concluding chapter we want to briefly compare the doctrines of assurance of Calvin and Barth. They have both points of contact and of divergence which we summarize below.

1. In both theological systems assurance is treated as a part of other doctrines. In case of Calvin it is the doctrine of faith, in case of Barth it is the doctrine of election. Both theologians realized that assurance cannot be sought and discussed directly and independently of other concepts. If one wanted to establish assurance concentrating on it as such he would certainly failed to reach his aim. The theology of the Puritans provides us with a historical proof of this thesis. Even such an admirer of Puritans as the pastor of the Metropolitan Tabernacle in London Peter Masters had to admit:

> Our tendency, sometimes, is to turn to more complex sources to find the real meat of the subject, such as the sermons of the Puritans. But in their sermons those great men tended to over-elaborate on the practical securing of assurance, proliferating categories and procedures which sometimes greatly complicate matters. One notable Puritan provided over thirty sermons on how to examine the conscience (to find evidence of grace within). His numerous observations are superb, and would helpfully engage a thoughtful pastor, but taken as a whole they go far beyond practical usefulness, and could even shake the assurance of susceptible readers (14).

Karl Barth's Doubts about John Calvin's Assurance

This underscores the genius both of Calvin and Barth who dealt with assurance so to speak glancing at it with side vision.

2. In both theologies assurance has an objective foundation. In Calvin – promise of Christ, in Barth – election of Christ. This Christocentric approach allows to escape the introspection of Puritanism which made self-examination the first and the last foundation of full assurance.

3. The Scripture is the basis of assurance in that sense that it gives us revelation about promise and election. There is a difference in understanding of the nature of the Scripture. Calvin simply equates the Bible with the divine revelation, with the Word of God. Barth understands the Word of God as Jesus Christ. For him the Bible is not divine revelation, it is only a trustworthy human witness to the revelation in Jesus Christ. Here, then, lies a subtle difference between Calvin and Barth. 'Subtle' because Barth used Bible *as if* it was inerrant (cf. Brown 146). 'Difference' because Barth would never recognize the Bible as such as the revelation from God and Calvin would never recognize such a Bible as the reliable witness to the promise of Christ.

4. The ultimate basis of assurance is different in Calvin and Barth because they understand reconciliation in different ways. Calvin understood the atoning work of Christ in terms of his sacrificial death and post-ascension intercession. Barth believed that atonement is accomplished by means of incarnation, that is, as the direct result of the hypostatic union between divine and human natures of Christ.

5. The ultimate hope which assurance gives is different. Hope in Calvin is continuation of life in a resurrected body. Hope in Barth is eternalizing of the life in the sense of the being-no-longer except in the mind of God.

6. Election plays the opposite roles for assurance. In Calvin – assurance of salvation is the basis of certainty of election. In Barth – election is the basis of assurance in salvation. Although as for assurance of the future, i.e. perseverance of the saints, both theologians regarded election as its basis.

7. Faith functions differently. In Calvin – assurance is part of faith. In Barth – assurance is not necessarily related to faith because faith is not the necessary

A Comparative Analysis

condition of salvation. In Calvin faith is knowledge of and trust in God's personal promise. In Barth faith seems to be more knowledge than trust.

8. Calvin and Barth agree on one not unimportant point: they both recognize the fact that men cannot believe in the gospel of themselves and that true faith originates in the work of the Holy Spirit.

9. Psychology of assurance is different. In Calvin – assurance is realistically mixed with doubt. In Barth – assurance is peace and pure joy separated from any anxiety and terror:

> The thought of God's predestination cannot, then, awaken in us the mixture of terror and joy which would be in order if we were confronted partly by promise and partly by threat. It can awaken only joy, pure joy... God's glory is revealed in the fact that He Himself removed the threat and became our salvation. In light of this end there is no place for anything but joy... This is not a matter of optimism. It is a matter of being obedient and not disobedient, of being thankful and not self-willed (174).

10. Finally and most importantly, Calvin's doctrine is based on the sound exegesis of the Bible while Barth's doctrine of election has an alleged biblical foundation but according to his critiques (Berkouwer, Brown, van Til) his exegesis is so innovative that it destroys the biblical witness. In other words we should come back to Calvin's teaching (after Puritan's relapse into works-oriented assurance) because it is based on the real biblical insight. And we must reject Barth's teaching not so much because of serious inner inconsistencies as because of its unbiblical nature. However interesting, fascinating, creative and thought-provoking Barth doctrine may be it cannot become part of Christian theology because the biblical foundation is lacking.

SELECTED BIBLIOGRAPHY

Barth, Karl. *The Epistle to the Romans*. Trans. Edwyn C. Hoskyns. Oxford: Oxford University, 1933.

---. *The Humanity of God*. Trans. Thomas Wieser and John Newton Thomas. John Knox Press, 1960.

---. *The Word of God and the Word of Man*. Trans. Douglas Horton. New York: Harper and Row, 1957.

---. *Church Dogmatics, vol. II/2*. 'The Doctrine of God'. 1942. Trans. Bromiley G.W. et al. Eds. Bromiley G.W. and Torrance T.F. Edinburgh: T&T Clark, 1957.

---. *Church Dogmatics: A Selection with Introduction*. Ed. Helmut Gollwitzer. Trans. Geoffrey W. Bromiley. Louisville: Westminster John Knox, 1994.

---. *Evangelical Theology: An Introduction*. Trans. Grover Foley. Grand Rapids: Eerdmans, 1963.

---. *The theology of John Calvin*. Trans. Geoffrey W. Bromiley. Grand Rapids: Eerdmans, 1995.

Battles, Ford Lewis. *Analysis of the Institutes of the Christian Religion of John Calvin*. Phillipsburg: P&R, 2001.

---. *Interpreting John Calvin*. Grand Rapids: Baker, 1996.

Beeke, Joel R. *The Quest for Full Assurance: The Legacy of Calvin and His Successors*. Carlisle: Banner of Truth, 1999.

Berkouwer, G.C. *The Triumph of Grace in the Theology of Karl Barth*. Trans. Henry Boer. Grand Rapids: Eerdmans, 1956.

Brooks, Thomas. *The works of Thomas Brooks*. Ed. Alexander B. Grosart. 1861-67. Vol. 2. Carlisle: Banner of Truth, 1980. 6 vols.

Brown, Colin. *Karl Barth and the Christian Message*. London: Tyndale, 1967.

Calvin, John. *Institutes of the Christian Religion*. Trans. Ford Lewis Battles. Ed. John T. McNeill. Philadelphia: Westminster, 1960.

---. ---. Trans. Henry Beveridge. Grand Rapids: Eerdmans, 1989.

---. *New Testament Commentaries*. Eds. T. F. Torrance and D. W. Torrance. Grand Rapids: Eerdmans, 1960.

---. *Sermons on the Epistle to the Ephesians*. Carlisle: Banner of Truth, 1973.

---. *Heart Aflame: Daily Readings from Calvin on the Psalms*. Philadelphia: P&R, 1999.

Cunningham, William. *The Reformers and the Theology of the Reformation*. Carlisle: Banner of Truth, 1967.

Dowey, Edward A. *The Knowledge of God in Calvin's Theology*. Grand Rapids: Eerdmans, 1994.

George, Timothy. *Theology of the Reformers*. Broadman Press, 1988.

Greef, W. de. *The Writings of John Calvin*. Grand Rapids: Baker, 1993.

Grenz, Stanley J., and Roger E. Olson. *20th Century Theology*. Downers Grove: IVP, 1992.

Helm, Paul. *Calvin and Calvinists*. Carlisle: Banner of Truth, 1982.

Masters, Peter. 'Gaining and Keeping Assurance' in *Sword and Trowel*, Jan.-Mar. 2003:14-20.

Packer, James I. 'Assurance'. *New Dictionary of Theology*. Eds. S. B. Ferguson, D. F. Wright, J. I. Packer. Downers Grove: IVP, 1988.

Parker, Thomas. *A Biography of John Calvin*. Philadelphia: Westminster, 1975.

Torrance, Thomas F. *Karl Barth, Biblical and Evangelical Theologian*. Edinburgh: T&T Clark, 1990.

Van Til, Cornelius. *Christianity and Barthianism*. Philadelphia: P&Reformed, 1962.

Wallace, Ronald. *Calvin's Doctrine of the Word and Sacrament*. Grand Rapids: Eerdmans, 1957.

Warfield, B. B. *The Works of Benjamin B. Warfield*. 1932. Vol. 4. Grand Rapids: Baker, 2000. 10 vols.

Westminster Confession of Faith. Glasgow: Free Presbyterian Publications, 1994.

Scientific Publishing House

offers

free of charge publication

of current academic research papers, Bachelor´s Theses, Master's Theses, Dissertations or Scientific Monographs

If you have written a thesis which satisfies high content as well as formal demands, and you are interested in a remunerated publication of your work, please send an e-mail with some initial information about yourself and your work to *info@vdm-publishing-house.com*.

Our editorial office will get in touch with you shortly.

VDM Publishing House Ltd.
Meldrum Court 17.
Beau Bassin
Mauritius
www.vdm-publishing-house.com

Lightning Source UK Ltd.
Milton Keynes UK
UKHW010641260421
382641UK00001B/102